Johan Schrøder's Travels in Canada, 1863

— ∴ —

D0209849

McGILL-QUEEN'S STUDIES
IN ETHNIC HISTORY
Donald Harman Akenson, Editor

JOHAN SCHRØDER'S
TRAVELS IN CANADA
—❖ 1863 ❖—

Edited, Translated,
and with an Introduction by
ORM ØVERLAND

McGILL-QUEEN'S UNIVERSITY PRESS

MONTREAL AND KINGSTON, LONDON, BUFFALO

® McGill-Queen's University Press 1989
ISBN 0-7735-0718-3

Legal deposit third quarter 1989
Bibliothèque nationale du Québec

Printed in Canada on acid-free paper

Publication of this book has been made
possible by grants from the Norwegian
Research Council for Science and the
Humanities and Multiculturalism Canada.

Canadian Cataloguing in Publication Data

Schrøder, Johan
Johan Schrøder's Travels in Canada, 1863
(McGill-Queen's studies in ethnic history; 5)
Includes bibliographical references.
ISBN 0-7735-0718-3
1. Canada—Description and travel—1764-1867.
I. Øverland, Orm, 1935-   II. Title. III. Title:
Travels in Canada, 1863. IV. Series.
FC72.S34 1989   917.1'044   C89-090334-4
F1013.S34 1989

To my parents Randi and Berge Øverland,
who introduced me to Canada

Contents

—— ❖ ——

Contents

Preface

When Johan Schrøder, a forty-year-old Norwegian gentleman farmer and agri-cultural journalist, decided to visit North America in 1863, his initial idea was to return after a few months and write a book that would be useful for the growing number of his countrymen who were planning to emigrate. After a relatively short time he changed his mind, not about writing his book, but about returning home to do it. Like so many of his fellow immigrants, Schrøder entered North America by way of the St Lawrence River and the port of Quebec, but neither Schrøder nor the majority of the others who came to Canada settled there. Throughout the nineteenth century the destination of most Norwegian immigrants, as well as those from other European countries, including the United Kingdom, was the United States, and Schrøder, too, even-tually settled in the region now called the Midwest. Before he did so, how-ever, he spent about two summer months in Canada – more time than most North American immigrants of that time did – and saw more of the country than most Canadians did in a lifetime. He enjoyed himself, was well received by strangers as well as by officials, and reacted positively to much of what he observed. In spite of this he chose to settle in the United States and advised others to do the same. Four years later, in 1867, he published *Skandinaverne i de Forenede Stater og Canada* (*The Scandinavians in the United States and Canada*) in La Crosse, Wisconsin. Another edition, which included only the chapters on Canada, was published in Christiania (now Oslo), Norway, that same year, and an abbreviated Swedish translation was published in Stockholm in 1868. Schrøder's account of Canada, published here in English translation for the first time, is the only narrative of travel in the Province of Canada by a Scandinavian and one of the very few written by a traveller from outside the English-speaking world. The narrative of Johan Schrøder's travels in Canada in 1863 may not only give us a view of Canada of the 1860s as it appeared to an educated Scandinavian but also help to throw light on why Canada was bypassed by most of the European immigrants who entered the port of Quebec in the mid-nineteenth century.

In this translation Schrøder's frequent misspellings of names, of persons as well as of places, have been silently corrected and current versions of Indian names have been adopted. Notes explain any other changes in the text and indicate English words or phrases that Schrøder himself used.

A research grant from the School of Arts, University of Bergen, enabled me to study material in the University of Oslo Library, while grants from the University of Bergen and the Norwegian Council for Research in the Humanities made it possible for me to study Canadian material at the Elizabeth II Library of Memorial University of Newfoundland. For many of the books I used I depended on the excellent and friendly service of the staff of the Inter-Library Loan division of the University of Bergen Library. The Archives of the Norwegian–American Historical Association at St Olaf College, Minnesota, kindly provided me with a xerox copy of Johan Schrøder, *Skandinaverne i de Forenede Stater og Canada* as well as other material I requested.

Helge W. Nordvik of the University of Bergen and Odd S. Lovoll of St Olaf College generously read an early version of my manuscript and offered intelligent and well-informed advice. Henning Siverts of the University of Bergen Historical Museum read the pages on Schrøder's Indian encounters and was very helpful in guiding me to sources of information on North American Indians. Johanna Barstad, librarian for the Norwegian–American Collection at the Oslo University Library, gave invaluable assistance in locating material that proved useful, as did Lars Erik Larson of the University of Wisconsin–Whitewater. I also benefitted from conversations with Gerhard P. Bassler and other historians at Memorial University. The institutions that helped me in providing illustrations for this book were all generous in their assistance. For their generosity and good advice I am in particular indebted to Erik Grung of the University of Bergen printshop, Hans Storhaug of the Norwegian Emigration Center, and Neil Morgenstern for introducing me to the work of photographer Knud Knudsen.

Without the support of my wife Inger this book could not have been written.

Canada:

En kortfattet Skildring af dets

Geographiske Beliggenhed,

Produkter, Klima, Beskaffenhed,

Opdragelses og Borgerlige Institutioner,

&c., &c., &c.

Udgivet ifölge Fuldmagt.

Oversat af A. Jörgensen.

· Trykt af St. Michel & Darveau,
No. 3, Mountain Street, Quebec.
1857.

Title page of the Norwegian edition of the official Canadian emigrant guide book, printed in Quebec and published in Toronto 1857.

Glem ikke Adressen: Prindsensgade No. 3, Christiania.

Børn under 1 Aar gaar frit. Desuden erlægger hvert Individ over 1 Aar 1 Spd. i Landgangspenge. I ovenanførte Fragt er indbefattet Ombordbringelse i Christiania, samt fornøden Brænde, Belysning og Medicin under Overreisen.

Fragten med Jernbanen fra Qvebek er fortiden for vogn Person:

til Chicago,	Illinois	9 Spd.	64 ß
Milwaukee,	Wisconsin	9	60
Madison,	do.	13	114
Monroe,	do.	70
La Crosse,	do.	16.17	42
Lansing,	Iowa	42
Winona,	Minnesota	60
Red Wing,	do.	19	102
St. Paul,	do.	20	96

o. s. v. Børn mellem 4 og 14 Aar betaler halv Fragt, hvorimod Børn under 4 Aar gaar frit paa de amerikanske Jernbaner.

Alt Passagersi medtages frit paa Skibet og, naar Gjennemgangsbillet kjøbes hos os, ligeledes, uden Hensyn til Vægten, frit paa Jernbanen i Amerik saalangt som Billetten lyder.

[...]

Efternævnte Emigrantskibe er fortiden af os anlagte:

Concordia, 247 Læster, Kapt. Christiansen Afgang: ank. 13. April 70
Roska, 325 , : Steen : , 20 .
med flere.

For Passagersi, som af de indskrevne Emigranter indsendes til os og ankommer til Christiania mindst 8 Dage før Indskibningen, skaffer vi frit Pakhusrum samt fri Transport fra Jernbanen til Pakhuset og derfra ombord. Fragten til Christiania maa være forudbetalt. Tøiet bør være tydeligt mærket med det Skibs Navn, paa hvilket man har indtegnet sig.

Christiania, i Januar 1870.

Det Norske Udvandrings-Selskab,

autoriseret for Emigrantbefordring.

Kontor: Prindsensgade No. 3.

Trykt hos H. J. Jensen.

Information sheet published by the "Norwegian Emigration Society" in 1870. Along with information on schedules, rates, and recommended luggage (for instance provisions for ten weeks) there is reference to "a Canadian law of June 1868 that forbids the landing of emigrants in Quebec or any other Canadian port unless they have the necessary means for the continuation of the journey through the country to the United States. Because of this law no emigrants will be accepted as passengers until they have either deposited the money for railway transportation from Quebec to Chicago or Milwaukee or have already purchased a railway ticket from there to a place in the United States."

Such warnings were published in Norway throughout the 1850s and 1860s, but without much effect. (The archives of Hedmarksmuseet, Hamar, Norway)

A view of Stavanger, Norway, as it looked when Christopher Closter returned to his home town in 1860-1 and brought with him colonists for the Gaspé venture, including his parents and other members of his family. (Statsarkivet, Stavanger)

Facing page: Emigrants leaving home. Illustration in the popular weekly *Almuevennen* 13 (No. 12, 23 March 1861), based on a drawing by Adolph Tidemand (1814–76). The original is in Nasjonalgalleriet, Oslo. Spring was the main emigration season and the accompanying text spells out some of the dire consequences of following the stream: "In a few days hundreds of our countrymen will say farewell to their family and friends and journey across the great ocean to a strange country where they in the future will build and live. This must be a grave farewell; for those who are leaving as well as for those who are staying behind will be pained by the thought that they may never see each other in this life . . . Some may become victims of illness after their arrival to the goal of their journey, as has happened to so many who have gone before; others may suffer want and have to work harder than they were used to at home, however difficult it may be for the Norwegian laborer to make a living for himself and his family; and should they be lucky and achieve better conditions than they had in Norway, some may be tempted by one of the many heretics that abound in America and leave the faith of their fathers and accept his false teaching . . . So the leavetaking must be bitter and the steps heavy to the waiting ship."

Almuevennen.

Et Ugeblad til Oplysnings Fremme blandt Menigmand.

No. 12. Løverdag den 23de Marts 1861. 13de Aarg.

Dette Blad, der udkommer hver Løverdag, koster 1 ß Numeret og forsendt med Posten 18 ß Kvartalet, Subskriptionen er bindende for et Kvartal eller 13 Numere. Expeditionen er i Pilestrædet 31 d,

Udvandringen til Amerika.

Om ikke mange Dage skulle Hundreder af vore Landsmænd tage Farvel med sin Slægt og sine Venner og drage over det store Verdenshav til et fremmed Land for der i Fremtiden at bygge og bo. Det maa være et tungt Farvel dette, og baade for dem, som reise, og dem, der blive tilbage, maa Tanken om, at de vel ikke saa hinanden mere at se i dette Liv, være saare smertelig. Ingen af dem veed, hvorledes det vil komme til at gaa de Bortdragende. Maaske blive Nogle af dem Offere for Sygdom efter vel at være ankomne til Maalet for sin Reise, saaledes som Tilfældet har været med saa Mange før dem; maaske komme Andre af dem til at henslide sit Liv under Nød og haardt Arbeide, haardere end de vare vante til i Hjemmet, hvor anstrengende det end tidt er for den norske Almuesmand at vinde Udkomme for sig og Sine; og om de endogsaa faa Lykken med sig og deres Kaar blive bedre end de vare her i Norge, saa maaske dog En og Anden af dem lader sig lokke af en af de mange Branglærere, som Amerika har saa mange af, til at forlade sin Fædrenetro og antage hans falske Lære. Og hvilken Ulykke da for dem, som det hænder, og hvilken Sorg for deres Paarørende og Venner! Saa mange Ting kunne møde dem og tilintetgjøre det lyse Haab, hvormed de drage bort. Og derfor maa Afskeden være bitter, og tung maa Gangen være til det ventende

Almuevennen.

Et Ugeblad til Oplysnings Fremme blandt Menigmand.

No. 48.   Løverdag den 26de November 1859.   11te Aarg.

Dette Blad, der udkommer hver Løverdag, koster 1 ß Numeret og forsendt med Posten 18 ß Kvartalet. Subskriptionen er bindende for et Kvartal eller 13 Numere. Expeditionen er i Pilestrædet 31d.

Et Billede fra Kanada i Nordamerika.

Af Udvandrerne fra Europa bosætte Mange sig i Kanada, der ligger i Nord for de Forenede Stater og tilhører England. Paa Billedet sees et Blokhus, der er beboet af saadanne Udvandrede eller Kolonister, og ved Siden deraf en Bigvam, som tjener indfødte Indianere til Bolig. En saadan Bigvam opføres af tre til fire Stolpe, der bindes sammen oventil og overtrækkes med garvede Hjortehuder. Tverdøver den anbringes Stænger, paa hvilke Stindene af de Dyr, som fældes paa Jagten, ophænges og tørres.

Om Indianerne i Nordamerika er fortalt i Bladets 10de Aargang No. 5 og 6.

Kjartan.
(Efter Munchs „Det norske Folks Historie.")
(Slutning.)

Da Kjartan efter en kort Overreise landede ved Hvitaa i Borgarfjorden paa Island, hørte han strax, at hans Fostbroder Bolle, der før var reist tilbage, havde benyttet sig af hans Fraværelse over den bestemte Frist til at indbilde Gudrun, at han ikke længer tænkte paa hende, men derimod skulde ægte Kong Olafs Søster Ingebjørg, saa at Gudrun, skjønt først efter mange Betænkeligheder og næsten truet af sin Fader og sine

GANGER ROLF fört af Capt. NYBORG.

The steam ship *Ganger Rolf* (built in 1856) by which Johan Schrøder and many other emigrants of the time travelled from Kristiania and Kristiansand to Hull on their way to Liverpool, the main port for passenger steamers to Quebec and Montreal. (Bergens sjøfartsmuseum, Bergen, Norway)

Facing page: "A picture from Canada in North America." Illustration in the popular weekly *Almuevennen* 11 (No. 48, 26 November 1859). The brief caption begins: "Many European emigrants settle in Canada, an English possession situated north of the United States. In the picture there is a log house inhabited by such emigrants or colonists and beside it is a wigwam that serves as a home for the native Indians." (See p. 141, n.2.)

Steerage passengers on the steamships crossing the Atlantic in the 1860s would use the deck for diversion whenever weather permitted. (Bergens sjøfartsmuseum, Bergen, Norway)

Facing page: "French Canadians in the Montreal market place." Illustration in *Skilling–Magazin* 26 (No 46, 17 November 1860) for extract from J.G. Kohl, *Travels in Canada* 1861), entitled "From New York and Canada." The first sentence is indicative of the positive tone of the article: "There is hardly any country where the benefits of freedom are more palpably in evidence than in Canada." The French population is singled out for special praise.

Skilling-Magazin

til Udbredelse af almennyttige Kundskaber.

№ 46.   Løverdagen den 17de November.   1860.

Fra Ny-York og Kanada.*)

Franske Kanadiere (paa Torvet i Montreal).

Der findes neppe noget Land i Verden, hvor Frihedens Velgjerninger viser sig mere haandgribeligt

*) Efter Athenæum.

XXVI Aargang.

end i Kanada. Landets oprindelige Besidder var som bekjendt Franskmænd, hvoraf der endnu bor en 26000, som under en mindre liberal Styrelse sikkert vilde være høist brysomme Undersaatter, der vilde

Three rural scenes from western Norway in the 1860s. Johan Schrøder pays much attention to the quality of the soil and other conditions for agriculture in his account of Canada. For emigrants from western Norway, even the poorest soil in the areas of Canada where settlements were attempted would be far better than the land they had left. Nor would the cabins they could set up during the first year necessarily offer much poorer housing than they were used to.

Above: A farm in Nordangerdalen, western Norway, in 1870.
Top right: A *husmann*, or cotter's cottage.
Lower right: Rural labourers in Hardanger, western Norway, taking a break for lunch. The soil consists largely of rocks and gravel.

(Photographer: Knud Knudsen. Billedsamlingen, Universitetsbiblioteket i Bergen.)

The barque *Sleipner* of Bergen (built 1856), which sailed direct Bergen–
Chicago via the St Lawrence River with freight and emigrants in 1862
and 1863 when Schrøder noted its achievement in his journal. (Detail
of a painting, Bergens sjøfartsmuseum, Bergen, Norway.)

PART 1
Introduction

—❖—

1

The Canadian Discovery of Norway

— ∴ —

The colonial government of the united Province of Canada had no immigration policy in the years immediately after it was established in 1841. From the point of view of London, immigration was still seen as emigration from the mother country to its colonies in all parts of the world. There, emigration policy was primarily a response to population problems in the United Kingdom, not to Canadian national needs. Officials of the Province, however, also tended to use the term "emigration" rather than "immigration" when referring to the movement of people into Canada, thus reflecting their dual allegiance as representatives of Canada but nevertheless servants of His, later Her, Majesty's Government in London. Gradually, in particular in the 1860s, "immigration" became a more frequently but never consistently used term, a shift in usage that speaks of a growing tendency to regard Canada as a country and not merely as a provincial and colonial receiver of excess population from the United Kingdom, the center of the Empire.

There were emigration agents in the ports of Canada as well as in the Maritime Provinces; in 1835 the Office of His Majesty's Chief Agent for the Superintendence of Emigration to Upper and Lower Canada had been established in Quebec. The main responsibility of the emigration agent in Quebec and his assistants, however, was the care of destitute emigrants from Britain and Ireland and not the framing or execution of any independent Canadian immigration policy. For many years until his death in 1836, Alexander Carlisle Buchanan, the first emigration agent in Quebec, spent every "summer meeting vessels and advising strangers who were sadly harried by dockside agents with unscrupulous suggestions to sell. Later he scouted out over the areas inland, prepared reports upon their possibilities for settlers, and corresponded with the home government, Poor Law Guardians, and private individuals from all parts of the British Isles" (Cowan 1961, 187). There was no change in either the duties or the dedication of his successor in 1838, his identically named nephew.

Immigration to the North American colonies reached its peak in the famine year of 1847, when almost ninety thousand departed from the United Kingdom for Quebec (of whom more than fifteen thousand died either during the horrors of the passage or in quarantine or hospitals shortly after their arrival). In the years immediately following, several changes in the migration patterns from the United Kingdom and other European countries brought about changes in the official attitude towards immigration in Canada.

The promotion and supervision of immigration and settlement in Canada were among the responsibilities of the new Provincial Bureau of Agriculture, established in 1852. Two years later, when the Colonial Office in London decided to discontinue the annual appropriations for the emigration agencies in British North America, the Province of Canada made its first regular appro-priation for the promotion of immigration to Canada. While the transfer of responsibility for the care of British immigrants was primarily an aspect of the gradual development towards a more independent status for Canada, the Canadian decision to involve the Provincial government in the promotion of immigration signalled a shift in policy brought about by a growing awareness that, while immigration to the United States as well as to the British colonies in Australia and New Zealand was steadily increasing, a diminishing number of immigrants were coming to Canada, at least with the aim of settling there. Indeed, the emigration agent's figures for arrivals to Canada and departures from Canada to the United States showed that in some years more than half of those who entered Canada merely moved on to the midwestern United States. While a mere five thousand left the United Kingdom for Australia and New Zealand in 1847, the pattern changed within the next few years so that for most of the 1850s the annual immigration to the colonies in the Pacific was from two to three times that to British North America. In the early 1850s the number of British and Irish immigrants to the United States was approxi-mately seven times the figure for Canada.

There had, of course, been immigration promotion from the earliest times, but with the exception of the unsuccessful mission to the United Kingdom of Dr Thomas Rolph, who had been appointed official emigration agent for Canada by the governor in 1840, such promotion had been in the hands of either private individuals and organizations or representatives of the govern-ment of the mother country, and the point of view was the solving of problems at home rather than the economic and social needs of the colonies. From 1854, however, the Canadian government initiated various schemes to attract immi-grants to the Province.[1]

It is only natural that the official promotion of immigration to Canada was primarily directed to the population of the United Kingdom, but a significant change in the pattern of arrivals registered by the emigration agent in Quebec suggested that other countries might also be appropriate targets for Canada's promotional efforts. While virtually no arrivals from other European countries had been registered in Quebec prior to 1848, more than seven thousand such arrivals were registered by the agent in 1852 and in 1853, and almost twelve thousand in 1854. Consequently, the agent of the Bureau of Agriculture who was sent to promote emigration from the United Kingdom in 1854 also visited the continent of Europe, and the first promotional pamphlet published by the Bureau of Agriculture that year was translated into German.

We need not speculate on why Germans were selected as an important target group. From the earliest period of settlement they had been the largest non-English-speaking population group in the British colonies in North America, and in the 1850s German immigration to the United States surged ahead of that from Ireland. More than 90 per cent of Canada's population was still of either French or British origin, but there were significant pockets of German immigrants and Johan Schrøder visited one of the German settlements in Canada West, Gravenhurst, in 1863. It is not so obvious, however, why Norway was also singled out for special attention in the Bureau of Agriculture's promotional efforts from 1856, when a twenty-four-page pamphlet was published in four languages: English, French, German, and Norwegian. While the largest edition – twelve thousand copies – was sent to Britain, the other editions were not significantly different in size: four thousand copies were sent to France, six thousand to Germany, and five thousand to Norway. Those four editions were revised several times in the following years and other promotional pamphlets were also published in those four languages.

It would seem that Norway, a small country on the outskirts of Europe with a population of about one and a half million, was receiving more than its due share of attention by Canadian authorities. Indeed, Norway was among the weakest and most insignificant of nations in Europe. It had only recently come into its own as a separate country in 1814, after centuries as a province of Denmark, but only to become the weaker partner of the dual monarchy of Sweden and Norway until full independence was achieved in 1905. The nineteenth century, however, was a period of growth for Norway, with population expansion and economic development, and one indication of this growth is that its relative emigration rate was surpassed only by that of Ireland.

Individual Norwegians had long migrated all over the world, as had members of other nations, and many had of course settled in other countries. Thus Norwegian seamen had deserted in Canadian ports, some to remain, others to sign on again, and other Norwegians, like the fifteen who took part in Lord Selkirk's Red River settlement in 1815, seem to have been prisoners of war who were recruited.[2] An isolated episode in 1825, when a sloop left Stavanger loaded with emigrants bound for New York, has come to symbolize the beginning of Norwegian emigration to North America, but shiploads of emigrants did not begin to arrive with any regularity until the mid-1830s, with slightly more than eighteen thousand departing from Norway between 1836 and 1850, according to official statistics. Norwegian emigration, however, took a significant leap in the 1850s and in the next fifteen-year period almost sixty thousand left Norway, most of them for the United States. Emigration from the other North European countries was still at a trickle, and this alone may explain why Norway seemed an interesting target for Canadian promotion efforts.

Along with this increase in emigration, however, there was also a shift in the main route of migration. While a mere 240 Norwegians had landed at Quebec in the 1836–50 period, Quebec began to receive a larger number of Norwegian emigrants than New York in the years immediately after 1850, with 7,510 sailing to Quebec in the three-year period 1851–3 compared with 4,550 to New York and Boston. The importance of Quebec as the main port for Norwegian emigrants destined for the United States became even more marked in the following years: of a total of 46,900 emigrants in the years 1854–65, 44,100 took the Quebec route (Blegen 1931, 349–51). Such a significant shift in migration patterns was bound to catch the attention of the Canadian authorities. In his report to the Legislative Assembly for 1854, A.C. Buchanan, Her Majesty's Chief Agent for Emigration, not only noted "the large increase of the Foreign emigration by the route of the St. Lawrence," but observed that "The Norwegian Emigration to the United States appears to have almost entirely ceased, having fallen off gradually from 3000 in 1852, to 91 souls, the number landed during the past year. The Norwegian emigration to this Continent appears now to be confined almost exclusively to this route, and the numbers have shown a steady annual increase since its commencement in 1850."[3]

The immediate reason for the supremacy of Quebec as the gateway for Norwegian immigrants to the North American continent was the repeal of the British Navigation Acts in 1849, which opened up the lucrative timber trade between Canada and Britain for Norwegian shipowners. The American historian Theodore C. Blegen has noted that "as early as 1850 Quebec customs house returns indicate that the Norwegian trade was becoming brisk, for of ninety-six ships listed, forty-four were Norwegian, almost all of which came in under ballast and departed with an 'outward cargo' of lumber" for British ports (1931, 351). Norwegian shipowners soon discovered that this traffic could be made even more profitable by filling their ships with immigrants rather than simply recrossing the Atlantic with ballast in the hold.

Christopher O. Closter, a Norwegian who had settled in Canada in the late 1840s and was later employed as an emigration agent in Buchanan's office, claimed credit for this development in the immigrant traffic between Norway and North America. In his section of the emigration agent's report for 1858 he explained that during the winter of 1850, when he would seem to have been in Norway, he had described "the facilities of the Port, etc. to the Norwegian Shipowners" and convinced them of the advantages of "landing their Passengers at Quebec." The advantages of combining the new opportunity to engage in the lumber trade from Canada to England with the one-way passenger traffic based on the growing emigration from Norway, however, were so obvious that the dominance of Quebec as a port of entry for Norwegian immigrants to North America was hardly due to the talks that Closter may have had with Norwegian shipowners. Indeed, so great were the advantages that, as observed by Blegen, it was possible to reduce passenger fares to Quebec. Throughout most of the 1850s and early 1860s Norway was the leading foreign nation in number of ships arriving at Quebec, with the United States as the only close competitor. Compared with that of Britain, however, Norway's share of the traffic from Quebec remained modest. In 1863, of the total of 1,661 ships entering at Quebec, 1,381 were British, while Norwegian ships had a virtual monopoly in the traffic from New Brunswick (Lower 1973, 239). As grain became an increasingly important commodity for the transatlantic trade, Montreal, too, had increasing calls of Norwegian ships from 1860, many of them arriving with emigrants (Worm-Müller 1935, 568).

Although the opening of the Quebec timber trade for Norwegian ships was an obvious factor in the shift from New York to Quebec as the major port of entry for Norwegian immigration to North America, another factor was the improved transportation systems, by river and by rail, through Canada to the United States in the 1850s. According to Buchanan's report for 1854, these internal improvements had made the St Lawrence route "the cheapest and most direct route to the Great West from Europe." To Buchanan, this transportation system, in addition to the protection against runners and confidence men that his office provided, was the main reason for "the steady annual increase in the amount of our foreign emigration." Buchanan frequently returned to the importance of transportation systems in the promotion of immigration, and in his report for 1856 he observed that "the increased advantage, as well as the superiority of the route by the St. Lawrence ... cannot ... be too prominently brought before the notice of intending emigrants from the United Kingdom, or continent of Europe" regardless of their eventual destinations. Thus the timber trade had made passage to Quebec at reduced fares available from many Norwegian ports while the convenient route to the West up the St Lawrence made Quebec a more attractive port of entry than New York in the 1850s and 1860s.[4]

The alleged "superiority" of the St Lawrence route, however, was not sufficent by itself to attract the emigrants from other countries to Quebec. Although Germans came to Quebec in significant numbers in these decades, they were actually outnumbered by the Norwegians. The efforts of the Canadian authorities to attract Germans, Heinz Lehmann observes, "failed to make the Quebec route popular among the Germans. All the German emigration guides that have come to my attention did, in fact, recommend the trip via New York even to those who wanted to settle in Canada. Perhaps rightly so" (1986, 20). The several attempts to establish steamship lines from German ports to Quebec in this period failed (Worm-Müller 1935, 569) and New York remained the main port of entry for Germans as well as for the emigrants from other European countries.

All traffic between Norway and Canada was on sailing ships and it could be two months or more before emigrants set foot on a Quebec dock. Conditions on board were certainly not luxurious, but accounts of some of the worst excesses, especially of the traffic with destitute emigrants from the United Kingdom do not necessarily reflect the state of affairs on all such ships crossing the Atlantic with emigrants. There was competition for passengers among the sailing ships engaged in the emigrant trade from Norway, as suggested by the many newspaper advertisements offering passage to Quebec each spring, and newspapers in Norway as well as Norwegian immigrant newspapers in the United States published reports of complaints made against individual captains or their ships. Indeed, when Johan Schrøder weighed the respective advantages of Norwegian sailing ships and British steamers based on his experience of the latter in 1863, one factor he pointed to was that "On sailing ships fitted out by Scandinavian owners the emigrants receive far better treatment from captain and crew than on the steamships of other nations."

After a six- to nine-week voyage in close quarters and with an inadequate diet, however, many naturally were weak on arrival and easily susceptible to illness and disease. Nevertheless, Norwegian shipowners, who were slower than those of most other maritime nations in making the transition from sail to steam, competed successfully with German as well as English steamship lines for the Norwegian emigrant traffic in the 1850s and 1860s. But English passenger lines were increasingly active in promoting their services in Norway through newspaper advertisements, pamphlets, and a well-organized system of agents and subagents. While Norwegian shipowners could offer lower prices, the English companies enticed emigrants with the promise of a short and comfortable crossing. Liverpool was the main port of departure for these lines, and a network of services was established to help emigrants on their way from Norwegian fjords and valleys, across the North Sea to Hull and other ports, and on to Liverpool by rail. This was the route chosen by Johan Schrøder in 1863, and by the early 1870s the majority of Norwegian emigrants were leaving their country by way of England and crossing the Atlantic on steamships (Worm-Müller 1935, 627).

This development, however, also meant the end of the epoch when Quebec was the main port of entry for Norwegian immigrants to the United States, since the British passenger liners increasingly had New York as their port of destination. Nordvik (1988) has argued that Blegen and other historians have exaggerated the impact of the emigrant traffic on the Norwegian timber trade from Quebec. Throughout the period 1850–75 a significant and increasing proportion of the Norwegian ships arriving at Quebec did not come directly from a Norwegian port and most of these came in ballast. Consequently, the loss of the emigrant trade did not have a negative impact on Norwegian participation in the Canadian lumber trade, which continued to be dominated by sailing ships. On the contrary, the Norwegian share in this traffic continued to grow and, in 1881, 27.8 per cent of the tonnage involved in the lumber trade from Quebec was Norwegian.

With such a relatively large number of Norwegians travelling through Canada in the 1850s and 1860s on their way to Illinois, Wisconsin, Minnesota, and other midwestern states, it is not unreasonable that Canadian authorities decided to concentrate some of their promotional efforts on Norway, regardless of the small size of its population. These efforts seemed to have had little immediate effect, however: Buchanan's report for 1856 estimated that 41 per cent of all immigrants entering Quebec had gone on to the United States, and the nationality that demonstrated the least interest in Canada would seem to have been the Norwegians, of whom practically all, Buchanan observed, were headed for the United States.

Among the measures taken by Canadian authorities to counteract this exodus was the passage of an act in 1858 aimed at the regulation and control of the agents of American railroads and land companies. But, clearly, more positive initiatives were required. The emigration agent's report for 1858 included a report from Christopher Closter, his Norwegian-born assistant. Of the 26,604 Norwegian emigrants who had entered Canada since 1850, "all passed through the Province, with the exception of some 300 persons remaining in Upper and Lower Canada." The assistant had "made inquiries relative to the pamphlet, on the subject of Canada, which was translated and printed in the Norwegian language, and sent home by the Government some two years ago. I could find no one of them that had ever heard or seen the pamphlet referred to in Norway." Moreover, he had been advised by arriving immigrants that "unless the emigrants become convinced of the real character of the Province before they leave Norway, it would be difficult to convince them after their arrival to settle in Canada, as this country has, in many respects, been misrepresented in Norway."

Indeed, the representatives of private Canadian interests were among those who were active in encouraging Norwegian emigrants to move on to the United States, and Closter expressed his concern about the effect of "the through ticket system which has been introduced in Norway" by the Grand Trunk Railway Company. This railroad policy, Closter observed, not only ran counter to Canadian interests but was bad business: "... could this people be induced to settle in the country, they would not only be a great benefit to the province, but would by their respective industry, bring to the Company an annual amount equal to the price they receive from the sale of through tickets, to the emigrants only once." Nor was Closter alone in his view on the effect of the Grand Trunk policy on Canadian immigration. When one of the select committees on immigration in 1859 questioned a representative of the Bureau of Agriculture and Statistics on the reasons for the decline in Canadian immigration, he, too, mentioned "the through ticket system of the Grand Trunk Railway, whose interest it is to convey passengers to the most distant points" (1859, App. 19). Considering the fierce competition for immigrants among the many conflicting private as well as public interests, it seemed that the only efficient way to entice Norwegians to choose Canada would be through personal representation.

In 1859 and 1860 three select committees considered the problem of diminishing Canadian immigration and their reports all recommend a more active promotion of Canada abroad. The second committee specified Christiania, the capital of Norway, as one of five ports where resident Canadian agents should be appointed (Gates 1934, 29).[5] The recommendations were strongly supported by Buchanan and in the spring of 1860, Helge Haugan, a Norwegian immigrant, was sent to Norway where he opened a Canadian information office in Christiania. However, he was not the first agent employed specifically to work among Norwegians, and settlements of Norwegian immigrants in Canada had already been attempted by the time he began his work in Christiania.

2

Early Norwegian Settlements in Canada

The history of Norwegian and other Scandinavian immigration to Canada properly belongs to the last decades of the nineteenth century and the early decades of the twentieth, when large numbers of Scandinavians entered the Canadian West from Europe as well as from the Upper Midwest of the United States. In his two-volume history, *Norwegian Migration to America*, Theodore Blegen gave his chapter on the Norwegian settlement attempts in Canada at the middle of the nineteenth century the appropriate title "Canadian Interlude" (1940, 357–82).[1] The first such settlement was in the Eastern Townships near Sherbrooke in 1854 and the last and most disastrous one was established in Gaspé in 1860. Their history was brief and not conducive to the promotion of Canada as an alternative to the midwestern United States as an area for Norwegian settlement. When Johan Schrøder travelled through Canada in 1863 there were no Norwegian settlements in Lower and Upper Canada; only scattered Norwegians here and there in towns and villages.

It all began in 1853 when two Norwegians found their way to Sherbrooke, the administrative headquarters of the British American Land Company. Wooed by a company that possessed vast tracts of land, they liked what they saw, and next June A.C. Buchanan, the emigration agent in Quebec, could for the first time welcome a group of Norwegian settlers who were not merely passing through on their way to the United States but who declared that their goal was the Eastern Townships: "A small party of from 50 to 60 Norwegians have acquired some property in the Eastern Townships, near Sherbrooke, and, from the steady and industrious habits of these people, I entertain great hopes of their proving a valuable acquisition to that important section of the Province, and, moreover, be instrumental in attracting to it other parties of their countrymen in succeeding years."

This group, all of whom arrived on the sailing ship *Flora* from Christiania, was a rather modest portion of the 5,663 passengers of the 39 ships that came to Quebec direct from Norway that year. Nevertheless, Buchanan, who had witnessed growing numbers of Norwegian immigrants disembarking at Quebec merely to be herded onto trains or steamships for through transportation by the omnipresent agents and runners of American land companies, state governments, or railroad companies, was greatly encouraged by this event, which he hoped augured a new trend in immigration. "This is the first party of Norwegians, of any consequence, who have established themselves in Canada, and their attraction thereto is attributed to the favorable reports which they had received from two of their countrymen, who settled in that district in 1853. Should they prove successful, and of which I have little doubt, we may look for a further addition to their numbers, during the ensuing season," Buchanan wrote in his report to the Bureau of Agriculture in December 1854. Nor was this merely wishful thinking on his part, for in addition to the evident impact of the letters home from the two who had acquired land in Sherbrooke in 1853, he was fully aware of the importance of the steady stream of correspondence from family and friends in enticing the majority of Norwegian immigrants to settle in the midwestern United States.

The British American Land Company, too, had reason to place great hopes in the success of the Norwegian settlement. The company had experienced a slump, with British immigrants moving on to the West and diminishing returns of land sales, and a study of the company's business in 1852 had concluded that it would be necessary to make extra efforts to induce settlers to buy company land in the Eastern Townships (Cowan 1961, 139). Now that the first Norwegians had settled there they foresaw a steady influx of Norwegian farmers and employed a Norwegian immigrant, Cornelius Helgenius Tambs, as agent.[2] There does not seem to have been any further Norwegian settlement in the area until 1857, when Buchanan sent "a few young men ... without means ... into the Eastern Townships for employment," and Tambs succeeded in persuading a shipload of ninety Norwegian immigrants to come with him to Bury from Quebec in 1857.[3] Clearly, more would have to be done by the Emigration Office in Quebec if significant numbers of the Norwegians arriving in the Province were to be persuaded to remain there.

Buchanan, weighed down by his many responsibilities in Quebec, had not been very successful in his own scattered attempts to divert Norwegians from their planned destinations in the United States. But then competition for customers was fierce among the emigrant agents on the Quebec docks. Letters and accounts of the crossing in those years all tell of the activities of the Norwegian agents representing American interests, and in his 1858 report Buchanan stressed the influence of these agents in pursuading virtually all Norwegian immigrants to travel through Canada to the United States. Karl E. Erickson, who crossed the Atlantic in 1853 and was employed as a clerk in Wisconsin's immigration agency in Quebec the next season, has given a firsthand account of the teeming and strongly Norwegian-flavored life that was the immigrant's first impression of the New World. The Wisconsin immigration office, headed by Elias Stangeland and with five other employees, was altogether a Norwegian affair. Their main competitor, John Holfeldt, was another Norwegian who represented the Canadian Great Western and other railroads (Larson 1925, 61n) and for a period in the 1850s also served as agent for the Norwegian violin virtuoso Ole Bull, who had embarked on a disastrous colonization scheme in Pennsylvania. Stangeland represented companies that took immigrants by way of the St Lawrence River, the canal, and the Great Lakes:

During the whole season while the emigration office was open, a constant strife and persistent warfare went on between the agents and runners of the various lines ... Each one claimed special advantages and general superiority for his line, and their sallies and broadsides furnished no end of fun to bystanders and loafers on the docks. At times, when a clinch seemed imminent, excitement would run high. Agents for other lines partook in the fusillade, which often quite bewildered and confused both captain and emigrants, making it difficult for them to decide what line to choose for their trip westward. As a rule the first move that a runner made was to corner the captain of an emigrant ship and try to gain his good will, for success hinged on this point. But an experienced captain was likely to have made up his mind beforehand ... Holfeldt had a great advantage of Stangeland and the other agents and runners in that he had much previous experience in the business from the past season, and was well acquainted and on good terms with many captains. Indeed, many emigrants ... had been told that the first person they would meet when they arrived at Quebec would surely be Holfeldt climbing over the rail of the ship, and the word proved true in many instances. (Erickson 1934, 69–70)

The competition between these two Norwegian–American immigration agents is mentioned in several letters from immigrants during the mid-1850s. One wrote home from Illinois on 8 July 1854 that "Stangeland was the first to come on board in Quebec, followed by a hunchback named Hornfeldt [*sic*]." The two immediately began to quarrel, because, "as you may imagine, they both wanted to serve their compatriots well." This group decided to accept Holfeldt's offer since it was "supposed to be the fastest" (NHKI MS), and, indeed, it would seem that Holfeldt had an edge on his main competitor. In a letter from 1853 an immigrant explains that even though Stangeland was the first to board the ship, the captain had made a previous arrangement with Holfeldt and consequently sent his passengers by his line even though it proved to be the more expensive alternative (Larson 1925, 61). Indeed, it would seem that Holfeldt ran much of his business in co-operation with the captains of the immigrant vessels. In the Christiania newspaper *Morgenbladet* (2 March 1861), for instance, he placed an advertisement for his ship chandler business in Quebec addressed to "all my friends among the Norwegian captains," and giving information on steamship schedules between Quebec and the ports lower down the river.

While the agents, runners, and interpreters who swarmed the Quebec wharfs to ply their trade on every new arrival from Norway may have given the wondering immigrant the impression that the New World was largely inhabited by his own kith and kin, those belonging to the other main group of foreign immigrants entering by way of Quebec, the Germans, would have received much the same impression from the agents who concentrated their efforts on them. Although a German interpreter or subagent had been in the employ of Buchanan's office since 1851, and a larger share of the German arrivals than of the Norwegian were regularly persuaded to settle in Canada, most of the Germans, too, went on to the Western states. There were objective reasons for the preference of the American Midwest to the forests of the Province of Canada, but to interested parties in Canada the migration seemed to be a result of the underhanded work of agents and runners. Seeing large numbers of their countrymen arrive every summer, only to be whisked away to the United States, a group of concerned "German inhabitants of the City of Quebec" presented a petition to the Legislative Assembly on 30 April 1856, "representing that the German Emigrants arriving at the port of Quebec are, by insidious manoeuvres and acts of intimidation, hindered from remaining in Canada, contrary to their inclination, and praying that means may be adopted to ensure to the said Emigrants the protection to which they are entitled." Every summer season Quebec was a teeming market where human beings were the main merchandise.

Working from cramped and inconvenient quarters in St Peter Street and with an inadequate staff compared to the combined total of agents and runners in the employ of other interests, Buchanan had a task made all the more difficult by his responsibility for the ill and the destitute. Not until the late fall of 1862, when the offices of the Chief Emigration Agent were moved to the former Custom House, was Buchanan provided with waterfront premises. Listing this move in his report for 1862 as one of several changes he had initiated in the interest of greater efficiency, François Evanturel, the new Minister of Agriculture and Statistics, noted that "By this change Mr. Buchanan is enabled to exercise a closer supervision over the emigrants, to give them information and assistance more readily, and what is of importance, to guard and protect them against 'runners,' who are now unable to make prey of them with impunity, being under the eye of the River Police, these latter being stationed at the emigrant landing place." Buchanan concurred, calling the move "a decided improvement." The 1862 Select Committee on Immigration had also recommended the building of sheds adjoining the administrative facilities for the accommodation of immigrants on arrival, and the next spring the Committee on Immigration specified "A second Shed, similar to the one now being erected, on the opposite side of the Wharf, for single women," among several "additional arrangements to be provided at the Old Custom House" (1863, App. 3). These and other improvements in the Canadian immigration facilities in Quebec had just been completed when Johan Schrøder visited them the summer of 1863.

Also present in Quebec by 1860 were representatives of the Illinois Central Railroad, interested not merely in passengers but in settlers on the land grants they had received from the state. Their Scandinavian agent, the Swede Oscar Malmborg, who was travelling in Norway and Sweden in 1860 and 1861, wrote to his employers that they would need to have agents in Quebec in order to counteract the Canadian emigrant agents "who spare no pains or expense in inducing the arriving to settle in the Canadas," and agents were duly sent. Apparently the experience of these agents was that a Norwegian would be in a better position to influence his fellow countrymen, and in the spring of 1862 the Illinois Central employed the Norwegian–American clergyman Abraham Jacobson to work among the immigrants arriving in Quebec, where he devoted "as much time to relief work as to directing immigration. Indeed, so valuable did his relief work become that the Canadian government made him a grant of money to show its gratitude, not aware that he was at the same time acting as immigration agent of the Illinois Central" (Gates 1931, 73, 77). For Buchanan, who gave Jacobson his full support, saw his duty to lie as much in the relief of misery as in the promotion of Canada.

On the whole, however, Norwegian immigrants, as observed by Nordvik, were "fairly well off, not least in comparison with the thousands of poor Irish that were streaming ashore in Quebec in the 1850s" (1988, 4). This fact had not missed the attention of Buchanan, whose office kept track of the financial transactions of immigrants on their arrival in Quebec. The report for 1858 estimated that the year's 2,656 Norwegian arrivals had brought "$57,104, principally by bills of exchange, [Norwegian] specie, and exchange," adding that it was impossible to estimate the amounts brought in gold. For the eight-year period 1850–8 an average of $32.56 in "bills of exchange and Norwegian specie" was estimated for each Norwegian arriving in Quebec, and Buchanan was particularly interested in committing immigrants with some start-up capital to a Canadian future. However, it was mostly immigrants with the means to do so who left for the midwestern United States, while the poor arrivals from Norway became both a burden for the Canadian emigration agent and, consequently, a main target group for Canadian immigration and settlement promotion. For even though his main responsibilities lay with the emigrants from the United Kingdom, Buchanan could not simply let the sick and the needy of other nations lie on the wharfs and streets of Quebec, and many Norwegians owed their lives as well as their passage to Iowa or Minnesota to Buchanan and his assistants.

The Canadian authorities were forced to take measures to avoid having Quebec congested with paupers, and whether an immigrant was given a ticket to a destination in Canada with the promise of employment or was simply put on a steamship or train for the United States, the end result was often the same: "All were provided with free transportation and meals from Quebec to their destination," Norman Macdonald writes of Buchanan's work, "nearly all of them re-migrated later to the United States" (1966, 72). While requests were made to British authorities to stop the practice of simply putting desti- tute immigrants on ships to Quebec, where they would have to depend on the charity of Buchanan's office, there were no official channels by which Buchanan could effect the migrations from other countries. In December 1854 Buchanan had sent an official notice to the Norwegian–American newspaper *Emigranten* in Wisconsin with the request that it be placed in newspapers in Norway. Here he announced that because of the increasing numbers of immigrants, from Norway as well as from other countries, who arrived without the means for further transportation, the emigration agency in Quebec was forced to limit all aid to the care and medical attention of the ill. Without excep- tion, all immigrants would be refused free transportation from Quebec and the notice gave information on the present cost of transportation via the Great Western Railroad. The notice appeared in Norway the following spring, for instance in *Almuevennen* 7 (1855, No. 5), but had little effect. Indeed, a similar notice signed by Buchanan was published in Norway a decade later (*Morgenbladet* 12 August 1865), and as late as 1868 the Ministry of Agriculture was still instructing its emigration agents abroad to warn immigrants "that no more passage money or land transport is to be given immigrants on their reaching our shore" (Loken 1980, 23). As long as Norwegian immigrants continued to enter the New World via Quebec, Canadian authorities were forced to come to their assistance.

A notice in the Norwegian newspaper *Stavanger Amtstidende og Adresseavis* (7 August 1861) throws light on the charitable efforts of Buchanan as well as on the way in which immigrant groups and runners deliberately exploited Canadian charity. When the Canadian-built and Norwegian-owned *Maple Leaf* docked at Quebec on 22 June, there were 198 passengers who claimed they "did not have a single cent." After eight days in Quebec they were given free passage to Toronto, where their interpreter then was able to raise $100 among them for further transportation into the United States. Apparently, then, Norwegian appeals to Buchanan for assistance could have been as much an expression of their wiliness as of their destitution. The correspondent explained the behaviour of this particular group of immigrants in Quebec as a response to the letters they had received in advance from family and friends in Wisconsin who had told them that, if they could only get to Quebec, they could count on being provided with free passage through Canada into the United States. That they later complained in letters home that the Norwegian runner had cheated them merely adds to the typicality of the story.

The cost of providing services and transportation to destitute Norwegian immigrants should not, however, be exaggerated. Not only were those who needed financial assistance a small minority, but the majority who paid their way through Canada generated far more Canadian income through their need for transportation and other services than the expenditures involved in taking care of those who were without funds. It should also be noted that Buchanan's efforts to provide transportation for the poor were not altogether altruistic. For instance, in July 1856, out of a total of 109 immigrants who received assistance from Buchanan's office, 21 were Norwegian, all arriving on the same ship from Stavanger. They were, wrote Buchanan in his report for that year, "all desirous of proceeding to the Western States." He, however, sent them "to the Buffalo and Lake Huron Railway for employment, and where laborers are much needed," adding that they "will doubtless proceed after their friends so soon as they acquire sufficient means."

Moreover, all assistance to immigrants was part of the general policy to encourage people to enter the country. The Province of Canada could have taxed the large stream of Europeans entering its ports, but in its eagerness to entice immigrants, the Canadian government did not tap the potential source of revenue that these immigrants after all constituted. While the accounts that Norwegian immigrants gave of their travel through Canada in numerous letters to friends and relatives in the old country never speak of any customs control on entering the country, the immigrant letters of the 1860s give advice on how to deal with the US customs officials who would be confronted at the border crossing. One explained that since a family could have seven members and the customs per family was $1.10, money could be saved by forming groups of seven; another advised immigrants to wear their new boots or shoes or hide them well at the bottom of the chest before meeting the American customs officer (NHKI MS, 24 June 1868; 17 July 1869).

Buchanan's office was not the only agency that provided free travel and other assistance to destitute Norwegian arrivals. In many of the immigrant letters from the period when virtually all Norwegian immigrants to North America came by way of Quebec, there are reports of how the agents and representatives of American-owned railway companies provided free tickets to the members of a group without means as one way of enticing the whole group to choose their transportation. A letter from Chicago in 1853 explains that "our captain made a contract for all passengers with the fastest and best line at eight dollars per adult and children under three free of charge, and 60 who were poor were also given free accommodations to whatever point they chose. All this was done for us by our good captain and he also distributed money among the poor and we owe him gratitude for his concern for us all" (NHKI MS, 1 September).

That this was a common practice is confirmed by Karl Erickson in his account of his work for Stangeland the following year. For immigrants without the necessary funds for tickets, Erickson explained that "provision was made by an agreement with the transportation companies, which carried them free on condition that the paying ones be sent over their line" (1934, 73). Buchanan was, of course, aware of this practice and was in fact competing with the American agents in providing immigrants with free transportation. In his report for

1856 he tells of a group of Norwegians who arrived on the *Gifion* in the second part of August. They were all on their way to Wisconsin, but sixty of them "stated they were without means" and "were offered a free passage to Ottawa City; with a promise of employment during the winter, if they would proceed to that locality; they, however, declined the offer, and as afterward informed, with the assistance of their fellow passengers, succeeded in obtaining sufficient money to enable them to reach Chicago."

The humanitarian assistance provided by Buchanan's office was nevertheless considerable, and the need to aid the poor, the ill and the helpless as well as the policy of attempting to persuade arriving emigrants to settle in Canada made it necessary to employ assistant agents and interpreters who could communicate with those arriving from countries outside the United Kingdom. A German assistant had been engaged in 1851, but it is not clear exactly when A. Jorgensen, the first Norwegian employed by the Bureau of Agriculture to handle promotional efforts in Norwegian and to act as interpreter in Quebec, was appointed. Jorgensen had been involved in the immigrant trade at least as early as 1853, probably in the employ of one of the several steamship and railroad companies competing for the immigrant trade, accompanying groups of immigrants up the river from Quebec (Jacobson 1941, 68). By 1856, when he translated the official immigration promotion pamphlet and other material into Norwegian, he was working for the Canadian government, and it was no doubt Jorgensen who penned the 1854 warning as well as the translation of the long announcement from the Canadian Minister of Agriculture, advertising three areas in Canada West, that was published in Norwegian newspapers in the fall of 1856 (*Morgenbladet* 2 November, 1856).

It was in the following year that Christopher Closter, who had been involved in various business ventures, first in Canada West and later in partnership with Jorgensen in Quebec, was added to the staff.[4] Jorgensen was also a ship broker in Quebec, and in 1863 his firm Jorgensen & Co. was frequently listed in the "Shipping Intelligence" columns of Canadian newspapers as handling agent for Norwegian ships. There would have been no conflict of interest between the agents' business pursuits and their official duties. On the contrary, their contacts with Norwegian shipowners and captains made them all the more useful as emigrant agents.

Closter immediately set about developing various ambitious schemes for Norwegian settlements on crown lands in Canada West, and after the summer season he went to Norway to promote immigration to Canada. In 1858 he was again at work in Quebec and now his efforts were mainly concentrated on adding to the already established settlements in the Eastern Townships, even though these were on British American Land Company land, which was more expensive than crown land. Although his report for that year included critical remarks about the lack of support he had received from the government, and even claimed that "I found myself very much surrounded by opposition" to the work he had been engaged to do, it must have given Buchanan sufficient reason to feel optimistic about the prospects for settling increasing numbers of Norwegians in the future.

The reported Norwegian population of 126 in the Eastern Townships is lower than the sum of immigrants reported to have settled there in the preceding years, and suggests that there had been a good number of transients among them. Closter, for instance, discovered that 30 of the 90 immigrants Tambs had brought to Bury in 1857 "had left last spring for the Western States ... influenced by parties from the West." But the American experience had evidently not corresponded to the rosy picture given by the agents and the Norwegians had not found their lot improved by their move. Consequently, Closter was "happy to say that some of them have now returned again to the townships, evidently convinced that their industry would be equally as profitable in this country as in the States." One reason for their return was the more favourable climate of Canada and they had already settled down in the Townships "amongst those who remained steady on their land" and they were now "doing well." Closter felt that their present situation, especially "considering the many disadvantages they at first had to contend with, as they were all destitute of means," "shows a remarkable advance to prosperity, for the future." They had all found employment sufficient not only to support themselves but also to enable them to clear land that gave a sufficient harvest for "the coming winter." Indeed, a few had "by their industry even made payments on their land." At a meeting Closter had called while visiting the Eastern Townships late that fall, "it was most pleasing to observe their feelings of contentment in their respective situations and a universal desire to adopt some plan whereby they could be able to bring others of their country people to join them in their adopted home."

Although the settlement in the Eastern Townships thus seemed to be prospering, it must be kept in mind that Closter would have had an obvious interest in painting as bright a picture as possible of the effects of his work. Even so, Closter included several observations that should have made Buchanan realize the precarious nature of the Norwegian settlements in Canada. Not only were the ubiquitous American agents to be reckoned with, but they actually had a point when they lured settlers with the prospects of cheap land. The $3.00 that twenty-five Norwegian families had paid for each of the three thousand acres they had purchased from the British American Land Company was not an extravagant price, considering the many advantages of the land, Closter explained; but it was nevertheless so high compared to the prices offered in the states in the West that he insisted it would be futile to expect large numbers of Norwegians to settle there "unless the Government would feel interested to set apart a tract of land in some part of the Eastern Townships, for the purpose of offering the Norwegian emigrants some additional inducements."

Indeed, in spite of their apparent satisfaction with their present situation, Closter had discovered that the Norwegians in the Eastern Townships were not entirely committed to their new country and they had "led me to understand, that circumstances may present themselves so to them, that they may think it for their advantage to leave" Canada. This would have a disastrous effect on all future attempts "to form another nucleus of the Norwegians in this Province, as this settlement ... constituted families from different parts of Norway." Closter, who well knew the importance of immigrant letters as a factor in the decision of others to follow after, warned Buchanan that all efforts "to turn the tide of the Norwegian emigration towards this country" depended on the success of this settlement since it would "establish the character of Canada in Norway."

In the official reports on Canadian immigration throughout the 1850s and early 1860s Norwegians were singled out for their alleged racial characteristics. But while they were consistently given attention far in excess of their actual importance to the settlement of the Province, the nature of this attention varied from praise of their qualities as sturdy, reliable, and hard-working, when the reports speak of the importance of retaining them as settlers in Canada, to writing them off as shiftless, ignorant, and work-shy when commenting on their departure after a season or two on the land. There is little reason to believe, however, that as a group they were either more sturdy or more shiftless than the settlers from the United Kingdom or the many German states. In her 1869 *History of the Eastern Townships*, C.M. Day, who makes no mention of Norwegians, observes of the "English emigrants of the poorer classes" who were brought to Bury by the British American Land Company that "many of this class of settlers become [*sic*] utterly disheartened, gave up in despair and left the place in search of other homes" (283–4). In giving up their heavily forested homesteads before they became productive, the Norwegian newcomers to Canada were merely behaving in accordance with a common pattern.

Indeed, the editor of the *Sherbrooke Gazette*, deploring the lack of interest in attracting foreign immigration to the Eastern Townships, especially "by our French Canadian fellow subjects," observed that all experience demonstrated "the imprudence of sending large numbers of emigrants in a body into the wilderness without anything with which to help themselves." Even though there were instances of the eventual success of such ventures, like the settlement of Scots in Winslow, the editor firmly stated that new settlers should not "be put through such a fiery ordeal" (29 August 1863). Surely, both Buchanan and his Norwegian assistants were fully aware of the precarious nature of all settlement attempts, in the Eastern Townships as in other parts of the Province of Canada.

Closter was re-employed as emigration agent in 1859 and continued his efforts to get Norwegians to settle in the Eastern Townships. While those who had settled there in 1858 had, in Buchanan's words, been "of the working classes, possessing but small resources," those who came in 1859, arriving with the barque *Brødrene* in July, seem to have been fairly prosperous. When Closter wrote his report at the end of the year he seems to have acquired more confidence in his position as well as an improved command of English:

Amongst the arrivals during the present Season some 15 families proceeded with considerable sums of money into the Eastern Townships; the remainder proceeded to the Western States. Those who went into the Townships purchased land there from the British American Land company, and amongst them were also three persons, who, it appears were sent out by their relations and friends for the purpose of selecting a locality for future settlement. These persons informed me, whilst I went with them into the Townships to examine the land, that the favorable appearance of the country far exceeded their anticipation, as they had been informed both in Norway and on their arrival that Canadian Lands, throughout the country were the most infertile for agricultural purposes in North America.

From a letter recently received from the Settlement in the Townships, I am informed that the three persons above mentioned, as also the others who proceeded there this Season, are well pleased with their selections, and expressed every confidence that it cannot fail to attract attention in Norway.

To all appearances, the Norwegian settlement in the Eastern Townships was on a solid footing. Everyone seemed to be employed, many had purchased land, and the work of clearing and tilling the land was progressing satisfactorily. Here, clearly, was a foundation on which the future promotion of Canada in Norway could be built. Buchanan's often-repeated observation that it would be a great advantage if more of the foreign immigrants could be pursuaded to settle in Canada before they left home had finally convinced the politicians of the need to send agents to Europe, and hopefully the combined effect of favourable reports from established settlers to friends and relatives back home and official encouragement and promotion from the Canadian government would now guarantee the growth of a Norwegian settlement in Lower Canada. The nucleus that Buchanan so often had maintained was a *sine qua non* for attracting large numbers of Norwegian immigrants to Canada had been established in the Eastern Townships.

The apparent conviction that the settlement in the Eastern Townships was a success and that government support as well as promotional efforts should now focus on other areas turned out to be a contributing factor in the eventual and resounding failure of all attempts to establish Norwegian settlements in the Province of Canada. By the fall of 1860, when representatives of Buchanan's office had ceased to visit them and new arrivals from Norway had been sent to other areas, Closter was already referring to "the unsuccessful settlement of Norwegians in Bury" and its negative effect on the image of

Canada in Norway. Nevertheless, when the 1859 Select Committee advised that Christiania should be the base for one of the two agents they proposed be sent to continental Europe, the promising results of the work of Christopher Closter, whose reports were available to them, were surely influential in their decision. Rather than concentrate on pursuing their success in the Eastern Townships, however, both Closter and Buchanan now had visions of a settlement of sturdy Norwegian fishermen in Gaspé. The story of that settlement is interwoven with the story of the work of the two agents Helge Haugan and Christopher Closter.

In the spring of 1860 Haugan, who had been a wagonsmith in Drammen and then after immigrating had tried farming for a few years in the Eastern Townships, set up office as a delegate of the Canadian government in the capital of his former country, just a short distance north of his town of birth. The instructions given him by the Commissioner of Crown Lands, P.M. Vankoughnet, specified "the districts of Sault Ste. Marie, Lake Nipissing, the Ottawa country, St. Maurice territory in the Eastern Townships, and Gaspé" as the areas where Norwegian settlements should be established, and he was cautioned, as were his fellow agents, not to misrepresent or make false promises (Gates 1934, 31; Blegen 1940; 368; Macdonald 1966: 81–3). He had been "entrusted with a number of maps and pamphlets in the Norwegian language, for distribution, and was employed to travel to the most important sea-ports and other Towns in Norway, to diffuse a knowledge of Canada," as Buchanan explained his commission in his report for 1860 to the Legislative Assembly. The same report gives an account of Haugan's work in Norway in his own words:

I opened an Emigration Office in Christiania, which I supplied with maps and books, and travelled also in the southern part, and by conversations, and explications of the maps, and the distribution of books, drew the peoples' attention to those advantages which emigration to Canada offers. I flatter myself that my exertions in these places will not be fruitless. I did afterwards make a voyage along the coast to Trondheim, which place I have now chosen for my station in the Northern part of Norway. On my voyage hither, I have, in all convenient places, communicated the necessary information, and distributed books and maps, so that every person who wishes it, could make use of it.

I have also, by my travels in the different land districts, attracted the people's attention, not only to the Farming, but to the Fisheries, and other useful occupations, and I believe thus, that a great number of Emigrants will leave Norway, next Spring, and settle the land district by the Ottawa River.

By constant advertisements I have also tried to encourage the important affair, and the enclosed extract, from a Trondheim newspaper, will show how my mission is understood at this place.

I have also, through letters, come in connection with people in Lofoten, Telemark and Vardø, and it is my intention to go thither in the month of February, when the fishing season commences, and arrange all the best way for them, and thus I hope to get many industrious, able and skilful people of this class to settle in Gaspé. Having seen that this is now a Free Port, I have instructed the people to bring their fishing tackle with them, as I am quite convinced this occupation will soon give occasion to constant and good work for many of the less wealthy when set agoing.

After the matter had gone so far, I determined to charter two Emigrant Vessels, one to leave Trondheim and the other Lofoten, and I am convinced that I have not only acted in the interest of the Imperial Government, but also in that of my emigrating countrymen. It is certain that the Norwegians, who live in a constant combat with nature, are a hardy, industrious and frugal race, well adapted to settle and cultivate a new country. I do also believe that the Canadian government, by inviting these people, have acted according to a higher inspiration, and that it will, in good time, gather rich fruit for its exertions.[5]

There is, however, no mention of the established settlement in the Eastern Townships in the report. Evidently the policy now was to concentrate efforts on the development of crown lands and let the settlement on the land of the British American Land Company take care of itself.

It is difficult to evaluate Haugan's performance as an emigration agent. He was received with suspicion in Norway, where the official view on emigration remained negative throughout the century and all voices of authority spoke discouragingly of leaving the fatherland and where newspapers and immigrant letters from the United States gave largely negative reports on the activities of agents and runners. In Trondheim, where he spent so much of his time, a local newspaper sceptically referred to him as "a person by the name of Haugan, who calls himself an agent of the Royal British Government in Canada," and described his efforts on behalf of the hundred or so labourers and artisans he had recruited as inept or dishonest or both (*Trondhjems Adressecontors-Efterretninger* 23 April 1861). Later that year another Trondheim newspaper had a report based on the correspondence of a member of the party of a hundred and fifty-five immigrants Haugan brought with him to Quebec and on to Bowman in Ottawa County where Haugan, assisted by Anderson, another agent from Buchanan's office, helped those who did not have the means to purchase land to find employment. The letter writer, however, had found the available employment neither secure nor to his liking and gone on to Chicago: "All who had some money have gone on to the western states, but those who had nothing had to remain."[6] He reported that Canada was not a good land for immigrants and that "the agents that the Canadian government to date has sent to Norway ... are very bad people in the way they deal with their emigrants, for they did all they could to cheat them" (*Throndhjems-Posten* 23 November 1861).

Under its new name, *Throndhjems Stiftsavis*, this newspaper brought more bad news the next fall when an artisan wrote home about the sad fate of many of those who were now struggling for survival in Chicago. He called Haugan, "who had persuaded them to leave Norway, a liar and a cheat," but it would seem unfair to blame Haugan for the trouble of those who, after all, had chosen to leave Canada (10 September 1862).[7] Moreover, for almost all immigrants, regardless of origin, the wages of the first years were hardship and misery, and those who complained and gave up seem to have expected instant success in a country where they were both unable to communicate and ignorant of all the essentials for getting on.

Whatever their reasons, however, the fact remains that the majority of the group that Haugan brought to Ottawa County in 1861 left within a year, leaving only forty-three. In his report for 1862 W.J. Wills, the emigration agent for Ottawa County, was nevertheless optimistic, noting that the Norwegians "appear industrious and frugal in their habits" and, moreover, that their "partial knowledge of lumbering operations would aid them materially in obtaining employment." Although there had been "great difficulties to contend with at the outset," he concluded, the Norwegian settlers now "appear sanguine of success." By the time he wrote his next report, however, it was all over: "The Norway element last year was entirely excluded from the Ottawa." The fault lay, he suggested, in the immigrants' lack of perseverance and their unwillingness to "give a fair opportunity to test the capabilities of the Ottawa."

Although Buchanan referred to him as "a very intelligent Norwegian" in his report for 1860, Haugan would seem to have been poorly equipped for the heavy responsibilities laid upon him by the Canadian government, and he may have made too many promises in spite of the admonition he had received from the Minister of Agriculture. He was, after all, merely an artisan from a small town in Norway whose main credentials seem to have been his Canadian residency and his own attempts to farm in the Eastern Townships. It is, of course, possible that he had political ambitions and that he was sponsored by the British American Land Company, on whose land he had settled. Gates not only notes that political influence was important in the not always felicitous selection of agents but "wonders whether some of the positions were not created to provide openings for office-seekers and whether one of the motives behind the demand for promotion of immigration was not the desire on the part of importunate office-seekers to obtain a sinecure" (1934, 34). Macdonald, on the other hand, discussing the 1860 appointments, concludes that "The persons chosen as foreign agents were carefully selected. They were favourably known and well-informed citizens" (1966, 82). Haugan was, at least to all appearances, honest and well-meaning, even though he may not have been well qualified as emigration agent or as farmer, a pursuit he soon gave up for a labourer's life in Montreal where, when Schrøder met him in 1863, he was making 75 cents a day. If, as H. Gordon Skilling observes, the early emigration agents abroad "deserve consideration ... as the earliest form of Canadian representation abroad and as the predecessors of later representatives more properly diplomatic in character" (1945, 2), then Haugan was certainly untypical in background, as well as in later career, of the persons usually recruited for diplomatic service.

Christopher Closter, who was even more maligned among Norwegian immigrants than Haugan, had an altogether different background. Not only did he have a net of contacts through his business pursuits in both Canada West and Canada East, but he was also well connected through his family in Stavanger, one of the early centers of Norwegian emigration. His ambitious plans to establish several Norwegian colonies in Canada were taken seriously by government officials, who seem to have been impressed by his work. Closter concluded his report for 1859 with a list of five "suggestions," the first of which was: "The Government to set apart three Townships for the exclusive settlement of Norwegians, in three different parts of Canada, namely, one on the borders of the Bay of Chaleur, one in the Eastern Townships, and one on the Northern shore of Lake Huron." On Buchanan's recommendation, land close to the village of Gaspé was selected for a Norwegian settlement: "In the development of the inexhaustible wealth which this country possesses in her fisheries along the seacoast and the Bay of Chaleur, the hardy fishermen of Norway might find a large encouragement; and fishing establishments, in connection with settlement, would greatly conduce to the general prosperity of the country," the Chief Emigration Agent noted in his report for 1859, taking his cue from the report from his Norwegian subagent.[8] Subsequent events proved them both wrong, brought ignominy on the name of Closter, and gave Canada such a bad name among Norwegians that they shunned the country until they began to spill over from Minnesota and North Dakota into the Prairie Provinces later in the century. "A total fiasco," is Schrøder's brief characteristic of the Gaspé project and neither his contemporaries nor later historians have given him much argument.

The development of Gaspé was by no means Closter's idea. In 1859 the Crown Lands Department had included the county of Gaspé in its survey of selected areas of Lower Canada and in his report for that year Commissioner Vankoughnet concluded that further roadbuilding and surveying in Gaspé "seemed auspicious for the advancement of colonization of that remote section of the Province." When they decided that Norwegians would be the ideal settlers for this remote section, Buchanan and Closter were merely acting on an accepted policy to develop the Gaspé region. Roadbuilding and surveying, Vankoughnet explained, continued with accelerated speed in 1860 as a response to "the rapidly increasing settlements ... which required an enlarged field for agricultural purposes." It would thus be a misconstruction to see the Norwegian colony in Gaspé as an attempt to settle unsuspecting and ignorant Europeans in a place that native Canadians refused to consider. Indeed, in his report for 1862, when the failure of the Norwegian experiment was an established fact, John Eden, the crown land agent in Gaspé, had apparently

forgotten his initial enthusiasm for a Norwegian colony and made full use of
the illumination provided by hindsight:

I cannot conclude this report without expressing my surprise at the efforts which are
being made, and the expenditure unhesitatingly incurred, in order to direct a portion
of the foreign emigration towards Gaspé, whilst we possess, in the province itself, the
best possible element for the colonization of that vast district. Every spring, from the
parishes of St. Thomas, Cap Ignace, Islet, St. Jean, St. Anne, Riviere Ouelle, &c, nearly
a thousand robust and active young men proceed to the Gaspé coast seeking engage-
ments for the fishing season. These are the settlers that should be encouraged to locate
themselves in Gaspé, and a little encouragement would soon induce them to do so.

While natives of Lower Canada were also leaving the province for the United
States in large numbers, it remains a fact that the Québécois were the only
group to form permanent settlements in the region. In their *Histoire de la
Gaspésie*, Jules Bélanger and his co-authors mention the Norwegian settlement
in Malbay as an example of the failed attempts to establish immigrant settlements, and observe that, by 1881, 95 per cent of the population of the counties
of Gaspé and Bonaventure was native to the Province of Quebec. With a total
of five inhabitants, Scandinavians formed the smallest population group registered by the census for that year (1981, 303–4).

The first two groups of Norwegian settlers had come to Gaspé from Quebec
in August 1860, accompanied by Closter, and under his guidance they decided
to acquire land in Malbay Township. Closter returned to Quebec after a few
weeks and filed an optimistic report with Buchanan, warning him, however,
that the lack of roads was discouraging and that, since the people had very
little capital, the settlement would need some public assistance during the initial
phase. The report concluded that the fifty members of the new settlement
were "perfectly reconciled to their new home." While Buchanan shared
Closter's enthusiasm for the project, there had been at least one cautionary
voice from the start. William Hutton, secretary of the Bureau of Agriculture,
had been suspicious of Closter's motives and seen him as a self-serving person;
he also had his doubts about sending shiploads of destitute Norwegians to
an isolated and undeveloped area in Gaspé: "I think you ought to take care,"
he wrote to Closter in Norway in the spring of 1861, "that these poor people
have no false hopes that the Can^n Gov^t will aid them" (Blegen 1940, 365, 370).

Meanwhile, Closter, armed with official letters of appointment as emigration
agent signed by Buchanan as well as by the governor's secretary, had set up
headquarters in his home town, Stavanger, where he could count on the support of his influential brother, Asbjørn Kloster, who had just launched the
first temperance movement in Norway. These letters spoke of dispensing information about Canada in general, even of giving advice to those who merely
wanted to travel through Canada on their way to the United States, and were

included in the advertisement that Closter, calling himself "travelling agent for the Canadian government," placed in several Norwegian newspapers as well as in his brother's temperance monthly. Here he announced the availability of lots from two hundred to fifty thousand acres on crown land in both Upper and Lower Canada.[9] Closter's heart, however, was in promotion of the Gaspé project: Not only did he plan to settle there himself; he also talked his elderly parents and a younger brother and his family into starting a new life in this eastern outpost of the Province of Canada.

Canada and Quebec had for a decade been familiar names to all classes in Norway. Along the coast, shipping and business interests were following the Canada trade with interest, every spring the newspapers carried advertisements for ships that would take passengers to Quebec, and there was a steady stream of letters (many of which were published in newspapers) to rural and working-class families from friends and relatives in the United States who had travelled through Canada. In the spring of 1861, soon after Closter's arrival in Norway, Canada became the subject of a widely publicized debate. Closter's advertisements had raised the ire of a conservative clergyman, Gustav F. Dietrichson, who had just returned to Norway after ten years of service among Norwegian immigrants in Wisconsin. He had met Closter in Quebec in 1859, and they apparently had had a disagreement on the immigration issue; now Dietrichson publicly challenged Closter to a debate on Canada as a land for Norwegian emigrants (*Stavanger Amtstidende og Adresseavis*, 10 January 1861). Closter was off elsewhere promoting his pet project and his brother responded on his behalf in the next issue of the newspaper, explaining that full information on Canada would soon be made available in a book that Closter was preparing for the press. The pamphlet that appeared some weeks later was essentially a revision of the official pamphlet that had been translated by A. Jørgensen, and although it did not give undue prominence to Gaspé, the area was described in favourable terms.

The attacks on Closter and the negative attitudes in the conservative press and among spokesmen for authority were not necessarily detrimental to Closter's efforts. From the very beginning emigration had been a popular movement warned against by officialdom, ecclesiastic and secular, and an emigration agent like Elias Stangeland was identified with the pietistic lay movement that was opposed by conservative clergy, as was Asbjørn Kloster's temperance movement. Moreover, the rural population had long paid more attention to the reports they received from members of their own class in America than to the warnings of their betters at home, and Closter soon received support for his promotion of Gaspé in the form of optimistic letters from Norwegians who had settled there the previous summer. These letters, written in November, were published the next spring in newspapers in Stavanger and, some days later, in Christiania (*Morgenbladet* 25 March 1861).

The glowing accounts often found in such correspondence must be used with caution by the historian. Immigrants could have had a psychological need to justify their radical decision to turn their backs on the fatherland or simply wanted to be joined by more friends and relatives. In this case, however, the positive accounts given in the letters are corroborated by Buchanan's report for 1860 in which he quoted from an optimistic letter he had received in November from Eden, the crown land agent in Gaspé, who had advised him "that the Norwegian settlers are making great progress, and appear to be perfectly satisfied with the lands they have taken for their settlement." The nine families had "six habitable houses of a good size" and the roadbuilding was making good progress. So pleased was Buchanan with this news of the prospects of a thriving Norwegian settlement in Gaspé, and so sure of the attraction this would have for future emigrants from Norway, that in November he sent a letter on Gaspé to the Norwegian and Swedish consul in Quebec, noting that each settler had purchased two hundred acres. The consul sent the letter on to the government in Christiania (Semmingsen 1941, 515).

In Stavanger the good news from Gaspé had spurred Dietrichson to action, and he advertised a public lecture on Canada (*Stavanger Amtstidende og Adresseavis* 20 March 1861). In this lecture, which was reported widely in the newspapers as well as in the popular Christiania weekly, *Almuevennen* (20 April 1861), Dietrichson advised against emigration in general, and against immigration to Canada in particular, and also warned against the work of agents like Stangeland and Closter. Although Dietrichson was moved by his class prejudices against emigration, he did offer clear-sighted criticism of the Gaspé project that should have been considered by Closter and his employers in Quebec:

The St Lawrence River is icebound during the winter and thereby isolates the inhabitants of Gaspé from the other populated areas. There are no cities there and no roads and if these have to be built by the settlers, as is to be expected, even if they get some support from the government, this will not leave them much time for fisheries or for the cultivation of their own land. If the land really is as good and as suitable for fisheries as Closter tells us, why has not such an excellent and felicitously situated area not yet been discovered by the many thousands of emigrants who come to Canada every year?

He also observed that the Canadian forests were not well suited to the settler without any means.

It would seem that this criticism had some effect; at least the ship that had advertised on 11 March that it would make a stop at Gaspé if there was a sufficient number of passengers for that destination advertised again on 27 March that there would be no stop at Gaspé (*Stavanger Amtstidende og Adresseavis*). Closter felt that he had to defend himself publicly and he advertised a public meeting at his brother's school in mid-April, a few weeks before the departure of the *Iris*, which was to take Closter and his followers to the promised land.

Dietrichson, too, made his appearance at the meeting and, judging from the newspaper reports, the exchange between them was mostly devoted to personal attacks and did not serve to clarify the question of Canada's suitability for immigration. Indeed, Closter undoubtedly had difficulty countering some of the points made by Dietrichson since in his earlier report to Buchanan he himself had observed that it would be necessary to connect the Norwegian settlement with the main road, and reminded the chief emigration agent that the Norwegians who had come to Gaspé did not have sufficient capital to develop the settlement. Nevertheless, the debate was so widely publicized that it served to make Canada even more of a public issue than it already had been.[10]

The sad story of the settlement in Malbay Township has been told many times, first in letters from despondent participants that were given wide circulation in the Norwegian press, then in a memoir and narratives based on conversations with survivors, and, later, by historians. To Blegen, the main problem, "in addition to difficulties of climate, land (especially the fact that the settlers were not able to secure tracts along the shore), and employment," was the lack of sufficient funds to survive the winter of 1861–2 (1940, 374). In spite of the troubles ahead, however, and apart from the scepticism of William Hutton, the beginnings were auspicious.

The first two groups to arrive in the summer of 1860 found everything to their liking and the letters sent home that winter were full of praise and optimism. An account signed by nine of the immigrants in November stresses the abundance of fish as well as the opportunities for those with experience from Norwegian fisheries:

The majority of the population here are engaged in the fisheries, which are very profitable. The great and famous Newfoundland Bank, that comes close to Gaspé and provides grounds for the coastal fisheries here, will no doubt prove a profitable field for those of my fellow Norwegians who have been used to fishing. The people here only use a single hook and line, so I would assume that Norwegian tackle would give a better catch. Consequently, we would advise any Norwegian who possesses fishing gear to bring this with him should he decide to come here. The herring fisheries are conducted in the same manner as in Norway, as are the great mackerel fisheries during the summer and part of the fall, and the trapping of lobster. Cod is prepared by the same methods as in Norway and is shipped to different places such as New York, Boston, South America, the West Indies, the Mediterranean etc. Fish is caught from May to late fall, herring in the spring and fall. There is also whaling and sealing.

Moreover, the two-hundred-acre lots they had purchased were adjacent to rivers where fish was plentiful and which offered power for mills. Land was reasonable and those who had their minds set on the United States were told to be aware both that land was scarce and expensive in the old Norwegian settlements and that the money saved on transportation west from Quebec would buy them a farm in Gaspé. Although lots were a few miles inland from the sea, lots for boat-houses on government land on a small peninsula nearby had been reserved for their use. The government was not only building roads but had promised to build a schoolhouse for the exclusive use of the Norwegians (*Morgenbladet* 25 March 1861). A reader today may well wonder at how lightly these correspondents dealt with the hardships of pioneering, the sweat and the aching muscles, the cold and the discomfort, as well as the primitive cabins that provided shelter for pioneers in the first years on their clearing, but it should be remembered that these were people used to a life of hard physical labour and few luxuries. The rosy picture they drew of Gaspé was an accurate rendering of their vision of the future wages of their labour.

The following summer they were joined by the group that Closter brought with him from Stavanger as well as by some of the immigrants whom Haugan had recruited in the Trondheim region and whose ship (the *Flora*, which in 1854 had brought the first group of settlers to the Eastern Townships) landed them at Gaspé, a group of Swedish Quakers whose leader was in correspondence with Asbjørn Kloster, and stragglers recruited on arrival in Quebec. Some, like the family of Nils Christian Brun, who were part of the group led by Haugan, had been influenced by the letters they had received from relatives or friends already settled in Gaspé. They all took land in Malbay Township, in the same area as those who had arrived the previous year. Since all the land on the coast had been taken, they acquired lots in the forest some miles inland and spread over an area of thirty to forty miles. They were all exposed to the hardships to be expected during the building of a new settlement, had their common share of illnesses and deaths, and suffered from homesickness and the sense of the contrast between the wilderness situation they would be in for years to come and the tight social support system they had left behind, but all this they must have been prepared for, at least in theory.

Gaspé did not appear at its best the summer of 1861. In his report to the Commissioner of Crown Lands, Pierre Fortin, "Magistrate in Command of the Government Schooner *La Canadienne*, engaged in the Protection of Fisheries, in the Gulf of St. Lawrence," claimed that it was the worst summer he had experienced in the seven years he had toured the coast: "Never, indeed, in this period, was the shipping season so bad — never were there seen such frequent storms, so much rain, and so many fogs, and never did the fall set in so early." The snow began to fall in October and in the period from 1 October to 24 November there were thirty days of rain or snow. To the exceptionally inclement weather was added a poor fishing season. When *La Canadienne* anchored in the Gaspé basin on 7 August for the third time that season, Fortin noted that the local cod fisheries "had been rather unsuccessful" and in his "Remarks on the Canadian Fisheries of the Gulf" Gaspé Bay is listed among "the places where codfish has been the most scarce in 1861." Of herring and mackerel he remarked that they were generally scarce that year. But available sources do not indicate that the Norwegians who came with Closter found conditions particularly harsh the summer they arrived, and it was with considerable optimism that they settled in for their first and the colony's second winter.

This optimism found expression in the two first letters to be published in Norway from those who had departed with Closter for Gaspé, first in Stavanger and a few days later in *Morgenbladet* (28 December 1861). Although the letters spoke of woe, Gaspé figured as the haven that finally provided safety and hope for the future after the misery experienced in the midwestern United States. The correspondent had been in Quebec for a couple of months but without means to go anywhere else and he asked for money so that he could go to Gaspé and purchase land "because there are the greatest fisheries that exist in the entire world." His second letter is dated "Malen By" (meaning Malbay Township) 1 November, and here he told of how he had left Quebec in May to look at the land but had returned ill to that city where he was eventually joined by his family. Evidently the Illinois Central agents had given them free passage, but Illinois had not been to their liking and the land prices there had been far too high. So they had all found their way back to Quebec and were now in Gaspé, where they were very happy to be: "Here there is an abundance of fish; two men in one boat can catch four barrels of split fish in half a day and there is a good profit." He had bought a farm and seemed satisfied with the terms. Not only were things going well in the settlement, this individual, at least, was happy to be there and not in Illinois. Whatever the motives of the writer, and he seems to have been worried about having enough cash to make the next payment on his farm the following summer, this is not a report from a disintegrating settlement.

Letters from members of Closter's own family also speak of satisfaction with their choice of future home. "I like Gaspé much better than any place I have been before," Bertha Kloster wrote to her sister in Stavanger late in October, "and I don't doubt you would do as well here as there" (Blegen 1940, 375). As late as 28 February, Endre and Ole Kloster were among the ten Gaspé settlers who signed a letter published in *Stavanger Amtstidende* on 28 April commending the captain of *Iris*, the ship that had brought them from Stavanger to Gaspé, for his skill and kindness. There is no suggestion here of any dissatisfaction with their lot.

The reminiscences of Nils Christian Brun (1911), who was fifteen when he came to Gaspé from the northern county of Nordland, also tell of the promising beginnings of the settlement. Even with the hindsight of subsequent failure, Brun wrote favourably of the landscape as well as the soil, told of his work as fisherman with two different skippers, praised the Canadian government for their efforts on behalf of the settlers, and was careful in his criticism of Closter. Life was no doubt difficult that winter of 1861–2, but not more than in most new settlements. The departures that began in the spring were apparently brought about mainly by a collective loss of faith.

In addition to the employment available in the fisheries, the government organized the building of roads and bridges so that the Norwegian settlers would have access to their lots, paying wages of from $1.00 to $1.25 a day: "It seemed to us," Brun wrote, "as if we were paid to work for ourselves."[11] They began clearing the forest and raising log cabins, and the completed ones provided shelter for all. Most seem to have had the necessary funds to get started. Brun's family bought a cow and hay for the winter, with a neighbour they acquired a team of oxen, and they sawed planks for further building in the spring.

However, the sudden influx of four hundred settlers, in addition to those who had arrived the previous year, in a small, undeveloped, and isolated community created some problems.[12] When the first snows came, the price of a barrel of flour was at $20 and before long it was not to be had at any price. But the Norwegian settlers, advised by Closter, had prepared themselves for this eventuality. He had gone from family to family in late August or early September and collected money to purchase flour and other necessities in Quebec, where the prices would be lower than in Gaspé. As the settlers waited for his return, all manner of rumours of his whereabouts were rampant, but finally, late in October, he arrived. For whatever reason, however, he only brought a small amount of the provisions he had taken money for (Brun believed that his family got food for $20 of the $70 Closter collected from them), and he charged Gaspé prices! He explained that he had much more but he wanted to come immediately with some of it and would return in a couple of weeks. This was the last time Closter appeared in Gaspé, leaving behind not only the many settlers who relied on him but also his aging parents and his brother's and his own family, including infants, one of whom died that winter. Some assistance was provided by the Canadian government, which purchased and distributed a shipload of corn to those in need.

Holand (1930), who exaggerates the suffering of the Gaspé settlers in his somewhat melodramatic account, suggests that they all left as soon as the ice broke up and steamship traffic began in the spring of 1862. This myth seems to have been established by the time Johan Schrøder penned his account three years later. As might be expected, however, considering the difficulties of settling accounts, the logistics of moving so many families with all their possessions, and the alleged poverty of them all, the exodus was gradual and must have lasted all summer. Moreover, it seems highly unlikely that the majority could have made such a move without some outside encouragement and assistance.

While the reminiscences of Brun speak of hard-working and well-informed immigrants, the official Canadian reports on the failed settlements present a picture of the Gaspé settlers that corresponds with Johan Schrøder's later characterization of the unsuccessful Norwegian settlers in the Eastern Townships. In his report for 1862 Minister of Agriculture François Evanturel comments on the failure of "the Norwegian colony which the late Government tried to plant on the banks of the St. Lawrence," explaining that since it was "composed of a class of immigrants who were poor, burthened with families, and unused to agriculture, they became of course, not withstanding the aid which they received from the Government, discouraged in a strange land, and betook themselves elsewhere to settle." After a year's opportunity for reflection, Buchanan also laid the main blame for the failure of the colony on the Norwegian settlers themselves in his report for 1863. For Buchanan, however, the fault was not to be found in their unfamiliarity with agriculture, he believed the problem was that "they were evidently more farmers than fishermen."

John Eden, the crown lands agent in Gaspé, who at an earlier stage had been so optimistic about the undertaking and had written in positive terms about the new settlers, now wrote that he had been "greatly deceived in the character of the last Norwegian emigrants, who proved to be but little better than paupers and not over fond of work, very dissatisfied with what was done for them, and expressing in strong terms their being deceived by the Government who, according to their statements, were to provide for them for two or three years in making colonization roads &c." Indeed, Eden now realized that the Norwegians were "of a rambling disposition, very similar to English Gipsies."[13] While the initial praise of the hard-working and reliable Norwegians may be seen as part of an argument for support of the colonization scheme, the later, more disparaging characterization was surely prompted by a need to shift the blame for failure, as is made explicit in Evanturel's insistence that "the charge of neglect, which has been brought against the Government in this behalf, is accordingly unfounded."

Although the provincial government could hardly be blamed for the failure of Norwegian settlements in Canada, it is nevertheless a fact that the original proposal was not followed through. When Christopher Closter first launched his plan to settle Norwegians in Gaspé in his report for 1859, he had also laid down several conditions that, except for the employment of settlers in road-building, had never been made government policy. Perhaps the most important condition he had laid down was the appointment of a government agent "acquainted with both English and Norwegian languages" to take residence among the settlers and give them advice and assistance. He had also suggested that "a free grant of one hundred acres" should be given "to each head of family" and that the township selected for settlement should be reserved exclusively for Norwegians for a period of ten years. But the Canadian government cannot be criticized for not making Norwegians the most privileged immigrant group in North America.

Available sources do not offer a satisfactory explanation of just what went wrong at Malbay. When Asbjørn Kloster discovered what had happened many months later, he was not only concerned for his parents but full of bitterness towards his brother who had betrayed such trust. In spite of his obvious short-comings, however, Closter seems to have been weak rather than a deliberate scoundrel. Moreover, he must have had considerable personal charm, for neither Brun nor the Swedish Quaker Charles Shieldstream spoke unkindly of him and both seem to have had dealings with him later.[14] But the fact remains that almost all of the Norwegians who settled at Gaspé did so on the recommendation of Haugan and Closter and they all relied on Closter for advice as well as for the means of survival. That he betrayed their faith in him was probably of greater consequence for the settlement than the actual sum of money that he disappeared with (a sum that he later apparently tried to repay). Losing their faith in Closter, they also lost their faith in Canada and the govern-ment he represented, and they left as soon as they could, not for Norway, but for the Norwegian settlements in the midwestern United States.

But neither the hardships of a new settlement nor the immigrants' sense of betrayal are alone sufficient to explain the fact that by the end of the summer there was not a single Norwegian reported left in Gaspé. If many were so poverty-stricken that they had known near-starvation during the winter, and if Closter had made off with such a large share of the colony's funds, how could each and all muster the confidence, not to speak of the actual means, necessary for the long journey from Gaspé to the prairie states? Surely all four hundred did not leave in the desperate manner described by Schrøder: rush-ing on board the first steamer in spring and somewhat cynically announcing that they had no money for tickets but intended to stay on board until they were landed at Quebec.

In his memoirs Brun (1911) noted that he and his family had met the Reverend Abraham Jacobson as well as Christopher Closter in Quebec that summer. The former held Norwegian Lutheran services in All Saints Chapel and, according to Brun, had come to preach and administer the sacraments among the Norwegian immigrants.[15] It is a matter of record, however, that Jacobson's main mission was a secular one: to persuade Norwegian immigrants to make Illinois their home and, more particularly, to purchase their land from the Illinois Central Railroad. He had come to Quebec with letters of recom-mendation from the Lutheran Augustana synod in Chicago, which gave him access to the home of the Episcopal bishop of Quebec. Twice that summer he visited the Norwegians in Malbay armed with a letter from the bishop that ensured him the assistance of the Episcopal clergy in Gaspé. Later in life he told his children that the Norwegian settlers there had demonstrated their hospitality and their respect for the cloth by feeding him meat, which was scarce compared to the all-pervasive fish, which he would have preferred to eat but politely refrained from requesting. (This desire to seek alternatives to an abundance of fish further suggests that the story of starving settlers in Gaspé needs some modification.) As authorized agent of the Illinois Central

Railroad, Jacobson would have had both an obligation to recommend resettlement and the authority to issue the necessary tickets. While he was enjoying the support and co-operation of his Episcopal brethren, for whom the settlement of Protestants in Catholic-dominated Lower Canada would be high on their list of priorities, Jacobson was doing his best to bring these wayward Norwegians back to the Lutheran fold in Illinois and other midwestern states. Jacobson's visits to the remaining Norwegians in Gaspé that summer were surely the most important factor in their eventual departure – paupers as well as those already settled in relative comfort in log cabins on cleared land.

John Eden, who was aware that an effort had been made to lure the Norwegians off the land, wrote in a letter to Buchanan, which the latter included in his report for 1862, that "There was evidently some secret agency in rendering them discontented with this place." The true nature of the Reverend Jacobson's mission to Lower Canada, however, remained unknown to the Canadian authorities and the Minister of Agriculture believed him to be "their reverend minister, who accompanied them to this country," and referred with confidence to "private letters" he had received from Jacobson that gave "a sufficient explanation of the causes of the failure of this colony from Norway" (report for 1862). However Jacobson may have explained the defection of the Norwegians, he surely did not admit to his own duplicity in cloaking his role as agent for the Illinois Central in clerical habit. There is no way of knowing whether Buchanan ever realized Jacobson's role in the failure of the Norwegian colony in Gaspé, but by the time he wrote his report for 1863 he had "reason to believe that inducements were held out to them by parties opposed to their remaining in Canada."

The Gaspé experiment marked the end of the first chapter of Norwegian settlement in Canada. According to the "Report of Mr. A. Jorgensen, on Foreign Immigration," appended to Buchanan's report for 1864, the main difficulty in attracting Norwegian immigrants was the lack of "a nucleus settlement, where the strangers might find people speaking their own language and where they are assured and protected by the presence of some countryman of standing and influence." The once-promising beginnings of such a nucleus, in Malbay, in Bury, and in Bowman, had all come to naught. For several years the continued promotional efforts of the Canadian government as well as those of the private land companies were made impotent in Norway by the legends of misery and failure at Gaspé. In 1867, for instance, an advertisement from the British American Land Company offering to set aside land in the Eastern Townships for an exclusive Norwegian settlement was met with harsh criticism in the press. The response to this criticism from the Christiania agents of the company was defensive and modest in tone, suggesting that they themselves did not have great conviction (*Morgenbladet* 4, 15, 21 February).

Against this background of failed official attempts to bring Norwegian immigrants to the country, the interest and hospitality with which Johan Schrøder was met on his tour of Canada may be appreciated. He was wooed by Commissioner of Crown Lands William McDougall; assisted by Chief Emigration Agent Alexander Carlisle Buchanan; given a pass on the Grand Trunk Railroad by its general manager, Charles J. Brydges; offered the hospitality and assistance of agents of the British American Land Company in the Eastern Townships and of crown land agents in Canada West; and welcomed as guest in the home of David Price, member of Parliament and head of one of the largest lumber enterprises in Lower Canada. Schrøder's reception reflects the continuing official interest in promoting the settlement of Norwegians in Canada. In return, he wrote a fair evaluation of agricultural prospects for the immigrant settler in Canada. However, he followed James Caird and other students of agriculture in North America in recommending the prairie land of the midwestern United States rather than the forest land of the Province of Canada for the pioneer farmer. After his tour of Canada, Johan Schrøder took the example of the unhappy Norwegian settlers in Gaspé and made the United States his future home.

3

Canada in Norway

By the time Johan Schrøder crossed the Atlantic in 1863 with the intention of writing a book about North America that could serve as an objective and well-informed guide for prospective emigrants from Scandinavia, the so-called "America book" was an established genre in Norway. These America books were essentially guidebooks written by emigrants or by visitors to North America and published in Norway. The contrast between these Norwegian America books and the early and mid-nineteenth-century travel accounts by middle-class and aristocratic European visitors to the United States and British North America is striking. The latter were addressed to an educated European audience disinterestedly curious about the New World, while the former were written for a largely rural population whose interest in America was practical and personal and whose eventual choices and decisions could involve total commitment to the new country. The title of the earliest of these books to appear, *Sandfærdig Beretning om Amerika, til Oplysning og Nytte for Bonde og Menigmand* (*True Account of America for the Information and Help of Peasant and Commoner*, 1838), by Ole Rynning, as well as its preface addressed to "Dear countrymen – peasants and artisans," are indicative of the author's intentions. The fact that its university-educated author wrote his manuscript in a rude log cabin in Illinois further suggests the gap between this kind of book and that based on notes taken while staying as a guest in well-furnished homes or the best-available hotels.

The practical intentions of Rynning and his many successors set their books apart from those written to describe various aspects of New World society and politics to educated Europeans: There is little in these Norwegian guidebooks to interest the person who wanted to learn more about institutions and polite society on the other side of the Atlantic, but much advice on the Atlantic crossing, essential luggage, wages and prices, job opportunities, the acquisition of land, and the whereabouts of Norwegian settlements. New York and Quebec were briefly mentioned as places of transition; more attention was paid to

the untilled forests or prairies. Some of these books were written by uneducated farmers or artisans and their brief accounts of the westward journey
are filled with naïve wonder at the marvels of the New World and they seem
to have experienced an entirely different country from that of the visitor who
was convinced of the superiority of Paris or London to the backwoods of
North America.

The differences between these two versions of the New World are also
reflected in the two kinds of presentations of news from North America in
mid-nineteenth-century Norwegian newspapers. In columns devoted to news
from abroad, whether from Italy, Britain, or North America, the reader would
find items concerning politics, armed conflicts, catastrophes, and culture. In
the columns with domestic and local news notices, however, with headings
indicating the place of origin for the item, such as "Stavanger" or "Drammen,"
there would also be news and other information concerning North America
based on either correspondence from emigrants or reports from returned emigrants. While the former news notices or articles would for instance be about
presidential elections or the Civil War, the latter told of life among emigrated
Norwegians and generally concluded with either warnings against emigration
or recommendations of the New World. Some examples of correspondence
from emigrants in Canada published in the newspapers were presented in the
preceding chapter. The impact of such letters on the popular image of Canada
in Norway was far greater than that of any of the official Canadian pamphlets
distributed in Norway or the occasional newspaper announcements of the
Canadian Bureau of Agriculture or private land companies, as for instance the
long announcement of new colonization roads and available crown land in
Morgenbladet 2 November 1856, and the announcement from the Canadian
Land and Emigration Company in *Morgenbladet* 2 October 1865.

As Buchanan was aware, letters home from a successful settlement had more
promotional value than any number of official pamphlets or travelling agents.
This was particularly true when promotional campaigns misfired, as had that
of the Hudson's Bay Company in the 1850s. Beginning in 1853, the Company
had advertised for trappers and oarsmen in Norwegian newspapers, and by
1855 fifty-five Norwegians had joined the Company in spite of the warnings
in the same newspapers about conditions in Canada. Letters home and in particular the reports of returned Company men told of unbearable conditions
and were also printed in the newspapers. By 1859 all had returned
(Semmingsen 1941, 444–6). Few newspaper readers in Norway would have
distinguished between the Hudson's Bay Company and the Province of
Canada.

The newspaper notices and articles based on emigrant correspondence were
classified as "domestic" news not only because they were date-lined the
Norwegian towns and villages where the letters had been received but because
they were about the life and conditions of people in North America who were

still considered to be Norwegian. Moreover, they concerned one of the most controversial of contemporary domestic issues: emigration. In 1862 there were, for example, Norwegian newspaper articles and notices about current developments in the Civil War in the United States based on sources in New York or London, while the newspapers' sources for accounts of the Sioux war in Minnesota were letters addressed to rural communities and villages in Norway that were often reprinted in more than one newspaper. Similarly, the many news notices of emigrant experience in Canada and the newspaper controversy on emigration to Canada were presented as domestic rather than foreign news.

Needless to say, the emigrant letters that found their way into the columns of local and national newspapers were few compared to the large mass of correspondence generated by the emigration movement. But it should be noted that most of these handwritten documents nevertheless functioned as publicly available newsletters about North America. Actually, the distinction between published and unpublished letters is not without ambiguity since letters from emigrants in North America were almost always shared with relatives and neighbours and often copied immediately on arrival and passed on to other readers and to people who would pass them to other communities beyond the local setting of village and valley. Since the mass of emigrants from Norway settled in the United States, however, even the letters of the 1850s and 1860s – the period when most Norwegian emigrants travelled by way of Quebec – express little interest in describing or giving information about Canada. Indeed, in these letters Canada is conceived of not so much as a country or even a place as simply a route, the road to the midwestern United States. Often less attention was given to this leg of the journey than to the much longer Atlantic crossing itself. Since the letter writers were naturally concerned with those aspects of their experience which would furnish advice to those who might join them in the New World and thus tended to concentrate on such practical questions as provisions for the journey and prices and wages in the midwestern United States, the word "Canada" was often not even mentioned in the account of their long journey. "I will begin my narrative with the first place where we stopped here in America, a town called Milwaukee where we landed after having passed the Great Lakes," a woman typically wrote to her mother on 29 December 1853 (NHKI MS). Others would mention Quebec simply as the first *American* city they came to and then move on to describe their arrival at their final destination, where they were often welcomed by relatives or former neighbours.

In the many accounts of the immigrants' journey through Canada, however, a few features stand out as those elements of a shared mass experience that were regularly communicated in the flow of letters that went from North America to rural Norway. For the passengers of a sailing ship that had been six to eight weeks at sea without fresh food, it is little wonder that the

Newfoundland Banks and the cod they had often fished there loomed large
in their experience of Canada.[1] Nor is it surprising that the first sightings of
land, often St Paul or other islands, are mentioned, nor that so many comment
on the beauty of the land on either side of the St Lawrence as they approached
Quebec. For many, the quarantine station at Grosse Isle below Quebec was
their first encounter with the new continent, and the experience of having
to wash themselves as well as the ship was novel enough to be given space
in letters home.

It may seem strange that these rural immigrants hardly wrote about Quebec
or Montreal as cities that in size alone offered such contrast with the villages
and small towns of their own experience, but so intent were they on their
rural goals in the midwestern United States that they seemingly did not have
much interest in what these cities might have had to offer them. Quebec and
Montreal, along with Kingston, Toronto, Hamilton, and Sarnia or Windsor
were merely names of stages on their route, at first by river and canal to the
Great Lakes, later and increasingly by rail or a combination of river steamer
and rail. As could be expected, the quality and the price of travel accommodations were more important than the country and its people, and difficulties
with luggage were frequently mentioned while there was not a word on
Canadian society. Thus writers who did not so much as qualify Canadian place
names with an adjective commented with wonder on the beauty and size of
the river steamboat, remarked on the Lachine Canal, and mentioned the
Victoria Bridge in Montreal. A single letter among the approximately three
hundred unpublished letters from these two decades in the archives of Norsk
historisk kjeldeskrift-institutt in Oslo (NHKI) stands out, not only in including
most of the Canadian motifs scattered through the many accounts sent back
to Norway, but in attempting some description of the country and even considering it as a place to live:

On the 4th day we passed Scotland and then saw nothing but heaven and water and
an occasional sail ship for 6 weeks and 2 days. On a Sunday with good wind we sighted
St Paul and several other islands and 2 days later we saw the American mainland. Then
there was great joy among all and after that, coming up the St Lawrence River, we had
head winds every day and after 14 days, on a Saturday evening the 16th July, we
anchored at Quebec, all of us quick and healthy and well satisfied. The approach to
Quebec up from the sea is very long, with a beautiful landscape, especially on the one
side. All the houses are white. On the other, or north side of the St Lawrence River
there was land to be had for nothing along with enormous forests. This land is not
settled on or cleared for several hundred miles, we were told. Then all agreed that that
was better than buying the high-priced land in Norway. This stretch reminded me of
Norway's mountains, even though it had wide fields. We met more than a hundred
large ships each day on the river, so it was a marvel to see how much lumber is shipped
from here. Quebec is a large city with many enormously large steamships.

... On the 19th we boarded the steamship and arrived at Montreal, the capital, in the morning of the 20th and we were told that we were 2 to 3 thousand passengers. At one o'clock in the afternoon we boarded another steamship and then sailed through 30 locks and each lock was about 12 feet high for this was a man-made canal not much broader than the ship's breadth except at a few points where it was broader so that two ships could pass each other. This canal is 50 miles long. The 21st we changed steamship for the third time in a town named Kingston. This steamship was large and wonderful, three stories high and with space for the 2 to 3 thousand people, very friendly people regardless of whether they went first or second class. We took this steamship to the town of Rochester, but we passed many towns that we do not have the space to mention and the land from Quebec and up the river was very beautiful and flat and very fertile and with this steamship we sailed 250 miles on a wide lake so that we could not see land on either side. We left the steamship at a little town called Hamilton. (NHKI MS, 1 September 1853)

Letters such as this, written with little regard to syntax or spelling, provided the main source of information about Canada for rural Norway.

While Norwegian newspapers printed occasional emigrant letters that related negative experiences or disasters, Canada hardly figured in the foreign news presented in the newspapers of this period. The illustrated popular weeklies and monthlies did publish a few feature articles, but when such items appeared – even in the period when Norwegian emigration to Canada was frequently discussed – they were not related to the current emigration question. The illustrated weekly *Almuevennen*, which gave a long summary of Pastor Dietrichson's lecture warning against emigration to Canada, also gave expression to its anti-emigration views by publishing emigrant letters that were full of regrets for having left the fatherland, and concluded with warnings against emigration. The feature articles about North America in general or the few specifically about Canada in *Almuevennen*, however, were either neutrally descriptive or positive in tone. Moreover, the interest was often in exotic aspects of North American life, with descriptions of Indians as well as settlers in the wilderness of Canada or the United States who were never related to the emigrated Norwegian yeomen and crofters whose letters were published in other issues.[2]

Another illustrated journal in Christiania that occasionally published features on Canada was *Skilling–Magazin*. A generous extract from the professional German travel writer Johann Georg Kohl's *Travels in Canada* was for instance published in 1860, and in 1862, the year before Schrøder's Canadian tour, it published a serialized survey of Canadian history and current conditions. A study of the information on North America available in Norwegian newspapers and journals, however, must conclude in agreement with Christopher Closter's lament, in his report for 1858, that while the United States "has become a subject of every day conversation in Norway, by means of newspaper corre-

spondence, and agents, constantly employed for that purpose ... with respect
to Canada, their information is very limited."

An exception to the rule that editors apparently saw no relationship between
the occasional feature articles on North America and the current issue of emigration, is the agricultural supplement of *Skilling–Magazin, Ugeskrift for norske
Landmænd* (*The Norwegian Farmers' Weekly*), which Johan Schrøder edited
from 1857 through 1860. Addressing himself to farmers, the class to which
most immigrants belonged, Schrøder as a matter of course selected material
that considered North America from the practical point of view of the agriculturist – for instance, a series on the agricultural advantages of the western
United States reprinted from a Danish source. The only series of instalments
that dealt specifically with Canada, however, was based on a book by the
English member of Parliament, James Caird, *Prairie Farming in America*
(No. 21, 26 May–No. 29, 21 July 1860).[3] Schrøder gave this series the title
"America. Where Would It Be Most Advantageous for the Norseman to Settle
in This Continent?" and the first two of the nine instalments presented Caird's
evaluation of Canada West and Canada East from this perspective. With
Schrøder's later literary efforts in mind, it is interesting to note that in his introduction to the series of instalments from Caird's book Schrøder commented
on the losses and tribulations of the many emigrants who too late discovered
that they had invested their capital as well as their health in inferior land:

Many a Norwegian has gone to the forest lands of America and broken his health cutting
trees and clearing land instead of settling some miles farther away on fertile prairie land
without forest, which is merely a burden if there is no market for lumber. This has
also been the fate of many an Englishman. He has gone north to the forests of Canada
because he wanted to cultivate land under the English crown in order to be protected
by his own laws, should the need for protection arise. But perhaps he nevertheless would
have profited more from choosing another country. This was understood by intelligent
men in the home country and individuals among them therefore decided to make the
journey to America at their own expense and then return to publish what they had
discovered, thereby being of great benefit to their countrymen. Such a man is the Englishman Caird. He travelled, looked into everything himself, and then wrote a book about
his journey that he has called *Prairie Farming in America*. It should also be of great
use for the Norwegian agriculturist who has decided to leave for America, and help
him to see whether he will profit by relinquishing the land of his birth and his old
memories for America (p. 163).

Thus Schrøder spoke highly of the very kind of endeavour he himself decided
to undertake several years later.

These serialized extracts from Caird's *Prairie Farming in America* include
the only disinterested appraisal of Canada as a land for the emigrant farmer
to appear in Norwegian prior to Schrøder's own *Skandinaverne i de Forenede*

Stater og Canada in 1867. Caird, who crossed the Atlantic in 1858, followed the conventional route of travellers through the Province of Canada. From New York he travelled up the Hudson to Albany and then by train to Montreal. He soon went on to Ottawa, spending most of his time in Canada in Upper Canada. The little he had to say about agricultural conditions in Lower Canada were of a negative nature: The land was infertile, the weather inclement, and the French Canadians and their cattle miserable. Upper Canada got much better marks, but although the soil was more fertile there, the work involved in clearing the forest as well as the relatively high prices for land made agriculture unprofitable for at least the first four years. It was reasonable, Caird explained, that so many emigrated from the Province to the open prairies of Illinois and other western states. There the advantages were not merely the easily cultivated and fertile soil but the well-developed transportation systems by rail, the Mississippi, or the Great Lakes, as well as low land prices and a rapidly growing domestic market for all agricultural produce. The reader of the instalments from Caird in Schrøder's agricultural journal in 1860 would have had no doubts that the message was to avoid the forests of Canada and settle on the western prairies of the United States.

Haugan, who arrived in Christiania just as these extracts from Caird's book were being published, must have been met with widespread prejudice against the country he had come to recommend. The following year, when he concentrated his efforts in the Trondheim region and Closter was stirring a public debate on Canada from his base in Stavanger, the reactions in the Norwegian newspapers to the work of the two Canadian emigration agents were largely negative. In 1862-3 the most important public debate in Norway about emigration in general and the traffic to Quebec in particular was initiated from Quebec by Buchanan (Semmingsen, 1941, 173-6).

In 1861 mortality on Norwegian sailing ships had been high, especially on those from areas where epidemics had raged the previous winter, and it had been necessary for the Norwegian and Swedish consul in Quebec to intervene in several instances where ships carried more passengers than allowed by Canadian law. A letter from Buchanan to the consul giving figures for deaths on specified ships and comparing these figures to the overall mortality rate, was forwarded to the Norwegian government and consequently published in *Morgenbladet* (8 April 1862). A Norwegian government bulletin giving extracts from the consular report as well as official Canadian warnings to Norwegian shipowners issued by Buchanan in January 1862 were widely distributed, and in January 1863 a controversial bill regulating international passenger trade was laid before parliament. This step was, as Semmingsen suggests, to no small degree instigated by the disastrous passage of the sailing ship *Amelia*, which had come to Quebec in 1862 with forty-nine passengers dead and one hundred and seventy ill on arrival.

As a well-informed intellectual and as a writer and editor on agricultural matters, Johan Schrøder was familiar with the current debate on emigration as well as the many publications on North America available in Norway in the 1850s and 1860s. He had his own personal reasons for leaving Norway in 1863, but the general interest in emigration, the dominance of Quebec as the port of entry for Norwegians seeking new homes, and the public debates on the relative merits of Canada and the United States for the would-be settler would have encouraged him to believe that there would be a good market in Norway for a well-informed book on both North American countries.

When he set about realizing his ambitious project of travelling through Canada and the United States and writing an objective account of his experience, he had two main models to emulate: the German Johann Georg Kohl for his lively and popular travel narrative that brought him readers all over Europe, and the English James Caird for his integration of an account of his journey with practical information of interest to the immigrant in need of advice on where to purchase land. Moreover, he would have been aware of the work of A.C. Buchanan in Quebec as well as of the well-publicized difficulties encountered by Norwegians in Canada. Schrøder would also have been familiar with the propaganda efforts of agents representing the Canadian government as well as public and private interests in the United States, and would have read the kind of promotional guidebook that he was to warn against in his own book, publications like Christopher Closter's Norwegian edition of the official Canadian pamphlet or Elias Stangeland's pamphlet promoting not only Wisconsin, his employer, but also the transportation company in which he had business interests.

4

Johan Schrøder and
His Book

Johan Schrøder was born in Christiania in 1824, two weeks after the death of his father, who had come to Norway from Denmark in his late teens in the lowly position of shop assistant but who in the course of a few years had acquired a law degree and a position as civil servant in the administration of the general staff of the armed forces. After a few years, Johan Schrøder's mother took a new husband from the upper ranks of the civil service. In spite of his solid social background, however, Johan Schrøder does not seem to have been very ambitious or to have demonstrated much diligence as a scholar. At least he broke off his studies after completing the preliminary one-year university course in 1845, and there is no record of his activities in the following decade.[1] By 1856, however, when both his stepfather and his mother were dead, he apparently came into an inheritance sufficient to purchase the fairly large farm Øvre Voll (now a race-track) in Bærum, some miles west of Christiania. Here he found his true vocation, living the life of a gentleman farmer, serving as president of the local Agricultural Society, an organization dominated by his peers, and publishing widely on agricultural matters.[2]

There is an obvious continuity in the interests that are characteristic of his work as publicist and editor and the central themes that emerge from his evaluations of agriculture and agricultural possibilities in his later book on Canada. In an essay entitled "Why Does the Norwegian Farmer Usually Make Such a Poor Living?" which ran in two issues of his agricultural weekly, *Ugeskrift for norske Landmænd*, in 1858, the first three neglected areas (in a list of twelve) are drainage, fertilizing, and crop rotation, all issues he returned to again and again in his journal as well as in his later critical comments on Canadian agriculture. He also frequently recommended keeping a daily record of work on the farm, and in three issues in 1860 he gave, as illustration, "The Diary of a Norwegian Farmer," a parallel to the fictitious "Diary" he gave of life on a new farm in Canada West in his book. His views on the importance for the farmer of having accurate accounts and the frequent agricultural accounts he presented as illustrations in his book on Canada also reflect an interest he had pursued for many years: His major publication before his book on North America was a practical guide to the keeping of farm accounts, an eighty-five-page pamphlet published in 1860. When Schrøder commented on farming in Canada he wrote as a professional student of agriculture.

However well informed his views on agriculture and farm management may have been, Schrøder nevertheless appears to have been an illustration of the often-observable fact that sound theory does not necessarily lead to sound practice. The immediate reason for his decision to visit the New World and write a book about his observations was the failure of his farming venture: On 4 July 1863, a few weeks after Schrøder left the country, there was a brief notice in the Christiania newspaper *Aftenposten* on the foreclosure of Øvre Voll. For Schrøder, who was not encumbered by a family, the prospects of putting the Atlantic Ocean between himself and wagging tongues and returning when the scandal had subsided with a book manuscript that would again ensure him the respect of his peers in Norway must have been attractive.

His journey to London the previous summer, when he visited the London Exposition as guide and interpreter for a group of Norwegian manufacturers who had received stipends from the government, may also have encouraged him to think of further travels. The first leg of both journeys, by steamship from Christiania to Hull, was identical, and the 1862 excursion probably suggested to him that he should take a passenger liner from Liverpool rather than go by sailing ship direct from a Norwegian port, as did most Norwegian immigrants at that time.

In going to North America as an escape from the ignominy of a business failure, Schrøder is representative of those of his class who emigrated in this period, many of whom left Norway because of some social disgrace or financial embarrassment. In his book he explained that he went as a steerage passenger so that he would be in a better position to give accurate information to the prospective immigrant. The real reason he as a gentleman shared quarters on board the steamship the *Bohemian* with a class he would not have mingled with at home, however, is more likely that he could not afford a better ticket. Indeed, he had counted on free passage across the Atlantic when he left Christiania.

The arrival of this unknown although ambitious steerage passenger in Quebec on 22 June did not create much stir in a city where most attention was given to the simultaneous arrival of the hapless passengers and crew of the wrecked steamship the *Norwegian*, salvaged and brought into Quebec by its sister vessels the *St Andrew* and the *Bohemian*. Schrøder, however, did get the immediate attention of apparently indefatigable A.C. Buchanan, the Chief Emigration Agent, himself one of the shipwrecked passengers of the *Norwegian* and busy making provisions for the several hundred who arrived without any of their belongings. In all probability it was the emigra-

tion agent who brought Schrøder to the attention of the press and who occa-
sioned the brief notice under the heading "Norwegian Emigrants" included
in the regular column variously called "Shipping Intelligence" or "Maritime
Extracts" in Canadian newspapers[3]:

Mr. J. Schroder, a Norwegian candidate of Natural Philosophy, arrived in the Bohemian
yesterday — his mission to Canada being to examine the country from St. Johns [*sic*],
NB, up the St. Lawrence, calling at Gaspé; thence up the Ottawa, and through the Far
West, for the purpose of reporting authentically to the government of his country as
to the best localities for settling Norwegian emigrants, of whom there are annually about
3,000 arriving. His object is of much import, and from conversation with him we are
led to believe his judgment will be impartial.

Whether prodded by vanity or by his practical sense, Schrøder was guilty of
some slight misrepresentations in his conversations with Buchanan and the
journalist, the least being his padding of his slender academic background.
Although the notice does not explicitly say that Schrøder was an official emis-
sary of the Norwegian government, such authorization is certainly implied
in his "purpose of reporting authentically to the government of his country."
This slight "misunderstanding" may help to explain the attention Schrøder
was given by Canadian officials and politicians as well as by private and public
land agents. It would hardly be fair, however, to regard him as an imposter,
and at least Schrøder lived up to the journalist's belief that "his judgment will
be impartial."

During his two-month stay in Canada, from his arrival at Quebec on 22 June
to his crossing the border at Sarnia in mid-August, Schrøder kept a diary in
which he made notes of his adventures and conversations as well as of his
observations of the land from an agricultural point of view. With a letter of
recommendation from Buchanan, Schrøder boarded a steamer for Montreal
and found himself surrounded by raftsmen on their way back to the lumber
camp after having brought their timber rafts down the river to Quebec. He
also made the acquaintance of two Abnaki Indians on their way home from
the winter hunting expedition, and spent several days with them in their village
on the St-François River. "Only a few days back," he wrote with a mixture
of wonder and self-admiration, "I had walked on the cobblestones of
Christiania and now I was about to venture out in the pitch-black night on
the frailest vessel ever devised and follow wild Indians to their remote retreat."
In the Abnaki village he was particularly impressed by Peter Paul Osunkhirhine,
who, apparently unknown to Schrøder, was a Protestant missionary and a
prolific translator of religious books into the Penobscot dialect of the Abnaki.
After a few days in the Indian village he went on to Montreal where the general
manager of the Grand Trunk Railway gave him a two-month travel pass on
all lines of the Grand Trunk.

He spent much time in the Eastern Townships, enjoying the hospitality of Cornelius Tambs, the Norwegian-born agent of the British American Land Company, studying the agricultural potential as well as some of the more spectacular aspects of social life, such as religious fanaticism and stage-coach travel. Back in Quebec, he visited the Minister of Agriculture and observed the emigration agents at work. He had realized that there were no Norwegians remaining in Gaspé and had changed his mind about travelling along the coast from New Brunswick. Consequently, he did not venture very far east, but soon returned to Cacouna where he boarded the *Magnet*, a steamship that made regular excursions with tourists and other passengers from Montreal and Quebec up the Saguenay River. In Saguenay he was befriended by the Norwegian–Swedish consul, David Price, at whose estate he stayed for several days after he had made the excursion up the Saguenay River, going to Lake Kénogami in a gig and traversing the lake by canoe to get to Lake St-Jean, the northernmost point of his journey. Here, and during his stay with David Price, he gave vent to his anti-Catholic prejudices and witnessed the celebration of the re-election of David Price to his seat in the Provincial Legislature.

After a brief visit to Portland, Maine, still using his pass on the Grand Trunk, he returned to Montreal and entered Upper Canada, where he spent most of his time in Orillia and the wilderness north of Lake Simcoe. He laid plans to follow Sandford Fleming on an expedition westward to the Selkirk settlement on the Red River and farther on to the valley of the Saskatchewan River, no doubt inspired by Caird's accounts of the vast region leased by the Hudson's Bay Company in *Prairie Farming in America* and by the English parliamentarian's reflections on the conditions for turning the territory over to Canada. Fleming, however, was frustrated in his surveying plans, and did not go west until 1872, so Schrøder decided to turn his attention to the United States. In mid-August he crossed the border, having admired the exploits of the Norwegian barque *Sleipner*, the second European ship to go the direct route from Europe to Chicago by way of the St Lawrence and the Great Lakes.

In his first weeks in the United States he continued his travels and his writing, but soon had to think of some sort of employment. Happily, he found there was a need for his journalistic experience in the Norwegian–American press.

The first newspaper among the Norwegian immigrants in the United States had appeared in Wisconsin in 1847, and when Schrøder arrived in 1863, the major Norwegian publication was the weekly newspaper *Emigranten*, then published instalments from Schrøder's book in progress, then called "An American Diary," announcing it as "A Book for Scandinavians at Home and published instalments from Schrøder's book in progress, then called *An American Diary*, announcing it as "A Book for Scandinavians at Home and in America" scheduled for publication later that same year.[4] Schrøder, however, does not seem to have got along well with the editor of *Emigranten*, one reason no doubt being that he had his own ideas about how a newspaper should be run, while the editor resented advice from a man who had been in America only a few months. Schrøder, not to be daunted, was soon planning his own newspaper with Frederick Fleischer, a fellow immigrant of similar background. On 14 January 1864 the first issue of their new weekly newspaper, *Fædrelandet* (*The Fatherland*) appeared in La Crosse, Wisconsin. Two of Schrøder's main interests are reflected in the contents of the early issues, which featured articles on agriculture and animal husbandry as well as extracts from his book in progress. The editors were rather ambitious, considering their readership of largely uneducated immigrant farmers living under frontier conditions, and they frequently published essays on history, philosophy, and similar matters.

Editing and publishing a newspaper, especially when a fire interrupted operations for several weeks early in the first year of publication, was a full-time job. Schrøder tried to travel through more of the midwestern United States settled by Scandinavians, but he soon realized that this would take too much of his time and limited resources. Moreover, his ambition now was to write an encyclopaedic description of the Scandinavian settlements rather than a book in which all information was integrated in a travel account, as in Caird's *Prairie Farming in America*. Consequently, Schrøder changed his strategy. On 11 January 1866 he published an open letter in *Fædrelandet* to "The Norwegian, Swedish and Danish Clergy in the United States and Canada," in which he requested specified information on Scandinavian settlements for his forthcoming book. By this time Schrøder had withdrawn from his position as co-editor of *Fædrelandet* and was concentrating his efforts on getting his much-delayed book published. As editor, however, Schrøder had already antagonized the largely conservative Norwegian–American Lutheran clergy, and it seems that he had few responses to his request for information.

Added to whatever suspicions there may have been concerning Schrøder's character as well as his qualifications were the vituperative polemics of the editor of the competing *Emigranten* who had once welcomed Schrøder's pen in his columns but was now making oblique references to Schrøder's business failure in Norway in his attacks on him and the rival newspaper, *Fædrelandet*. On 22 February Schrøder again placed an open letter in *Fædrelandet*, this time addressed "To the Norwegian People in America," in which he complained that he had had no co-operation from the clergy and requested the same kind of information from laymen in all settlements.[5] The attempt to involve as many correspondents as possible in his project was of course also a good marketing device, and Schrøder had earlier (14 December 1865) placed a lengthy and detailed "Invitation to Subscribers" in *Fædrelandet*, wherein he offered to list the names of subscribers in the book for an extra 25 cents. Eventually four hundred and forty-three seem to have paid for this honour. The financial success of Schrøder's publishing project was further secured by the soliciting of advertisements that take up eighteen pages in the completed volume, more than half of this space bought by railroads.[6]

Schrøder's "Invitation to Subscribers" raised the ire of the editor as well as the printer of *Emigranten*. The latter, Ole Monsen, had begun his own Norwegian publishing business, and when Schrøder began advertising his projected work on the Scandinavians in America, Monsen launched a counter-advertising campaign that was entirely destructive in tone and intent. Making his ads parodies of Schrøder's in *Fædrelandet* and using quotes to ridicule Schrøder's somewhat bombastic style, Monsen pounced on Schrøder's device of offering to print the names of subscribers in the book for a fee of 25 cents and offered "the Scandinavian Population of the United States" the opportunity to subscribe to a "Name Almanac" in which all who so desired could have their names entered for a mere 10 cents. Schrøder must have been dropping words about his next-contemplated, but never-realized, project, a history of the Civil War, for Monsen added a note in one of his ads: "If this speculation goes well I plan to publish a History of the War next summer so that the old country may realize that we exist. I may not know much about the war, but I intend to translate bits and pieces of what I may find. I will also approach Petroleum B. Nashby [*sic*] and Artemus Ward for contributions, and for the rest I will take as much as I want from larger works."[7]

Ironically, one sentence in Schrøder's advertising that the editor and the printer of *Emigranten* held up to ridicule was: "Let us show our countrymen in the old country that the Scandinavians in America have the strength and ability to publish books that the old country must take home from America to be informed." In fact, Johan Schrøder's *The Scandinavians in the United States and Canada* was the first book to be published in Norwegian in the United States and then be republished in Scandinavia. There is no way of knowing how many copies were sold in America, in Norway, and in Sweden, but having a book appear in three countries and in two languages was no mean achievement.

However, by the time the book appeared, four years after Schrøder had set out on his voyage, Norwegian interest in Canada had subsided. The Norwegian publisher who had acquired the rights to the book decided to publish it in two parts, first the Canadian chapters and then, a few months later, the rest of the book dealing with the United States. In an attempt to cut potential losses, he also invited subscriptions to the work while the first volume was on press, promising that those who had subscribed by the time the first volume was off the press would receive both volumes. Subscribers seem to have been few and the appearance of the first volume on Canada did not create a significant demand for the rest of the work, and the second volume was never published.[8]

Although Schrøder's more practically oriented and catalogue-like chapters on the United States may have been of most use to the emigrant seeking information on where to go and how to get there, and on the whereabouts of other

Scandinavians in the United States, there can be no question that the Canadian narrative is the more lively part of the book and the one that holds most interest for a reader today. It is also the part that remains closest to Schrøder's original plan of publishing his "American Diary." Even though some sections have been amended and comments added as he was bringing the book to completion during the winter of 1866–7, most of it retains the freshness of his first impressions and of his notes written in the evening after a day's adventures. The shifting point of view in the completed book between that of the recently arrived Norwegian traveller in Canada and that of the more Americanized editor in Wisconsin can be seen in the frequent changes in tense from present to past as well as the occasional implied comparisons between the two countries.

Schrøder's cultural and religious prejudices, however, were not much affected by the time he had for reflection in the years that passed from his first notes to his final editing of the book. But these prejudices, which appear offensive to present-day readers, are reflections of his time and culture rather than of his personal character. They find expression in his condescending description of the appearance as well as the religious services of "the sons and daughters of Erin" who boarded the *Bohemian* at Londonderry.[9] But above all, Schrøder's prejudices come out in his comments on French Canadians in general and their clergy in particular. In this respect, Schrøder's views were in harmony with those of the majority of Anglo-Saxon travellers in the Province, of whom Gerald Craig has observed that "a lack of sympathy, fortified by anti-Catholic prejudices, pervades the accounts given of the *Canadiens* along the St. Lawrence" (1955, xvi). An exception to this rule may be found in the German travel writer J.G. Kohl, whose Protestantism was also elsewhere tempered by tolerance. The very passages in which Kohl wrote lovingly of the friendliness and strong sense of place and family among the French Canadians had been among the extracts presented in *Skilling–Magazin*, the Christiania publication with which Schrøder had been associated, in 1860. Here, for instance, Kohl had observed that the French Canadian's love of family had led to a diminishing size of farms, since there was a tendency to divide the land so that offspring could remain on the land with their parents. Schrøder, however, remarked laconically on the fact that "Englishmen and Americans were invariably in possession of farms from 100 to 300 acres while the French were satisfied with 50 acres. The former think of their children's future, the latter only for themselves." Uninfluenced by his German colleague, Schrøder was more inclined to share the views of James Caird on the French Canadians as well as on the Catholic clergy.

Although Schrøder's prejudices are far from original, two of his confrontations with Catholic French Canada are so revealing of how preconceptions may block understanding that they deserve some comment. While sharing tight quarters in a canoe on Lake Kénogami with a Catholic clergyman, Schrøder was insufferably conceited as he tried to convince his fellow passenger of the delights of matrimony and the good example of the married clergy in an idealized Arcadian Norway. The priest, judging from Schrøder's own account, behaved with exemplary discretion and when he politely interrupted Schrøder's lecture, Schrøder felt he had scored a victory over this "poor Catholic who had forsworn womankind."

An equally glaring misinterpretation is apparent in Schrøder's description of the two processions in Chicoutimi, the home of David Price on the Saguenay. One was a religious procession in honour of the visiting Roman Catholic bishop, the other secular, in honour of the recently re-elected David Price, whose control of the district has been compared with that of a feudal lord. To Johan Schrøder, the popular religious procession in honour of the church and its representative was a sham, while the political demonstration of the many dependents of the all-powerful Price family was simply regarded as a colourful tradition. Schrøder's observation that the horsemen in the church procession were poorly dressed suggested to him a shameful lack of propriety; whereas he saw the simple fare offered as refreshment to the participants in the political demonstration as an indication of the relative poverty of the population. Such failures of understanding, however, were the failures more of a culture than of an individual.

In the light of such cultural blindness it is all the more remarkable that Schrøder, self-admittedly influenced by his youthful impressions of James Fenimore Cooper's noble savages, could have recourse to a sort of cultural relativism in his observations on the Indians. In his account of his days in a Western Abnaki village there is no reason to doubt his sincerity when he talked of his respect and his sense of friendship. In view of the fact that he had just stepped off the ocean liner, his relaxed and trusting acceptance of the two Indians' invitation to leave the river steamer and enter their canoe in the middle of the night suggests that he was more adventurous than the average traveller in Canada in this period. Considering his subsequent meeting with a small band of Maliseets at Cacouna, it is more important to note his understanding of the plight of the chief confronted with the white man's hunting and fishing regulations than his somewhat prurient interest when speculating on the presence of so many women compared to the small number of men. Indians should remain Indians, however, and not take on European airs. Schrøder thought that the Indian women he later saw in Orillia, dressed in the latest fashions, were ridiculous.

Even though he completed his book in the United States, Schrøder pointed to the better relationship between government and Indians in Canada and advised his countrymen that if they dealt fairly with the North American Indian, they could expect to be treated with respect in return.

His social prejudices in general were more pronounced when he was on the south side of the border, as for instance when he wrote about "the immodesty of young people" as a trait he came across in Canada but "discovered as a way of life" in the United States during his excursion to Maine. When, at the completion of the Canadian leg of his journey, he crossed the border into the United States, he exclaimed that he was now in "the land of fixers, guessers and snufflers." These are all characterizations that reflect an adopted "English" reaction to American usage, whereby "fix" is a verb of many uses, "guess" is a convenient recourse in a society in which opinions should be hedged, and a tendency to speak through the nose prevails. Even after he had committed himself to the United States, he thought of it as a country that had lapsed even further from a European ideal than Canada.

Some lapses, however, seemed to be North American rather than specifically of the United States, in particular the levelling influence of a society where land was plentiful and labour was scarce. Schrøder was servēd stories of the "haughty, lazy, and ignorant" behaviour of servants in Canada and he warned his readers that "families from Europe who are used to the comforts provided by good servants will have to relinquish this service in America." However, while similar comments on servants abound in Canadian travel narratives, Schrøder was also able to see the implications of this situation for those at the other end of the social scale, and pointed out that "poor emigrants who take work as servants in order to make a living on arrival will discover that this work is without comparison more comfortable, easier, and more profitable than in the old country." But what need did a society have for the "comforts provided by good servants" when eating, as observed by Schrøder, was generally regarded as something to get done as quickly as possible? Several times he returned to the general lack of table manners in his account of his Canadian journey.

But conditions for homesteading and the relative quality of soil were, finally, more important than manners or accents when a choice of country had to be made. And here Schrøder left no room for doubt: Although Canada may have had better farming land than even the best parts of Scandinavia, its forest land could be compared with the fertile and easily cultivated prairies of the midwestern United States. He nevertheless wrote more favourably of Canada, particularly Lower Canada, than most writers of the time. Indeed, Gerald Craig has pointed out that when Canada was considered as a land for immigration, the attention of most travel writers of this period "was usually confined to Upper Canada" (1955, xxviii). Schrøder was atypical both in spending so much of his time in Canada East and in giving it at least as strong a recommendation as Canada West. He had done his homework, however, and was fully aware of his minority position: "This view of the advantages of western Canada is apparently different from that of most other travellers, but the reader will have to judge for himself on the basis of my experience."[10] While in the United Kingdom the main interest in British North America had traditionally been focused on the areas not dominated by a French population, the few Norwegian settlements that had been attempted in Canada had been in Lower

Canada, with the exception of the small group that stayed for some months in the vicinity of Ottawa. It is only natural that Schrøder showed more interest in the Eastern Townships, where there already was a Norwegian history of sorts, than in the forests of Upper Canada.

Not only was Schrøder's point of view different from so many of the other travel writers; he had also chosen a different point of departure from that of most British travellers in Canada. Again, the current flow of Norwegian immigration by way of Quebec explains why this was natural for Schrøder. Craig points to the choice of most British travellers of "the more comfortable voyage to New York or some other American port, in preference to the Quebec route; they then frequently travelled up the Hudson River and across up-state New York to Niagara Falls, the great mecca of all visitors to North America. Apart from a hurried trip to Montreal and possibly Quebec, such an itinerary, probably ending again at New York, did not allow for extensive rambling through the lower province" (1955, xvii). If Schrøder went to see Niagara Falls, however, he made no record of it. It might be spectacular, but for the immigrant it was as irrelevant to an evaluation of the country's agricultural possibilities as were descriptions of cities. While Craig observes that few who wrote accounts of their travels in Canada "saw more of French Canada than its two famous cities" (xviii), Schrøder makes clear that "since Quebec is so decidedly not the place for immigrants to linger, a description of this city or of the other cities of America are outside the scope of this book." In his preface (which has not been included in this edition) Schrøder explained that his book was "primarily addressed to the agricultural class," since nearly all Scandinavians who immigrated to North America did so with the intention of becoming farmers.

However, in eventually coming out in favour of the United States as the land to which immigrants should go if they wished to farm, Schrøder was voicing a consensus opinion. Caird had done so in his *Prairie Farming in America* and as soon as Schrøder had the opportunity of seeing prairie land for himself in Illinois, he, too, was convinced:

To me it is now obvious that wherever the climate is not detrimental to health or agriculture, prairie land should be preferred to the best quality hardwood forest land. The poor settler will find an abundance of pasture and meadow on the prairie without sticking a shovel into the soil. He may produce his own milk and meat from the very beginning and set about tilling the soil. On forest land he would consider himself lucky if he succeeded in clearing and cultivating forty acres during his first ten years, while on the prairies it would not be difficult to plow forty acres during his first year. How far he then would be ahead of the settler on forest land after ten years!

But the quality of the land was not the only aspect to be considered, and Schrøder made clear that in Illinois the land was too expensive and that the immigrant had to go farther west, to Iowa or Minnesota, in order to get good land at a low price.

Even though Kohl had not been very interested in the prospective immigrant's perspective, he did raise the question of why there were so few Germans in Canada, and found it reasonable since better soil was available in Iowa and Minnesota. However, he pointed to another reason so many bypassed Canada that Schrøder did not mention: the immigrant's suspicion of the British monarchic system of government. Such a suspicion was surely in the minds of many Norwegian immigrants, and in his report to the emigration agent for 1858, Christopher Closter had mentioned their "spirit of Republicanism" as the explanation that many Norwegian immigrants gave for the lack of interest in Canada. As late as 1896 a Norwegian who published an account of a journey to Illinois by way of Canada to visit relatives and friends wrote that he "was favourably impressed by Canada and thought that its nature would be suitable for Norwegians. It is a shame, though, that the country is under English dominance. As long as this is the case people will be wary of going there" (Sollid 1896, 43).

Johan Schrøder's little book may not reveal many hitherto-neglected facts about Canada in the 1860s, but he does provide us with a refreshing point of view. An abundance of travel literature exists that gives first impressions of life and conditions in the Province of Canada, but almost all the accounts known to us have been written by travellers from the United Kingdom or the United States. In his bibliography Gerald Craig has only two travellers from continental Europe who paid more than passing attention to Canada before Confederation: the German J.G. Kohl, who travelled in the 1850s, and the French Duc de La Rochefoucauld-Liancourt, who visited Canada in the 1790s. With Johan Schrøder's account of his travels in Canada in 1863, a Scandinavian contribution is added to the few accounts of the Province of Canada by continental European travellers.[11]

Johan Schrøder's later career can be dealt with briefly, since he never wrote about Canada again. For some years he continued to launch new book and periodical projects aimed at a Norwegian readership in the United States, but nothing came of his ambitious plans. He was editor of two short-lived Norwegian newspapers in Minnesota; he also tried farming there. His political ambitions took him as far as to the office of Assistant Secretary of State in Minnesota and an appointment as United States Consul in Costa Rica in 1885. After his tenure as Consul was over, he tried farming for a few years in Costa Rica and then became a civil servant in that country's Bureau of Statistics, in San José. In this position he finally wrote the kind of official guidebook he had so readily disclaimed thirty years earlier: "by order of the Supreme Government of Costa Rica" Johan Schrøder's *Costa Rica. Immigration Pamphlet ... A Guide for the Agricultural Class Coming from Other Countries to Make Costa Rica its Home* was published in San José in 1893.

Skandinaverne

i

de Forenede Stater og Canada

med Indberetninger og Oplysninger fra
200 skandinaviske Settlementer.

En Ledetraad

for

Emigranten fra det gamle Land og for

Nybyggeren i Amerika

af

Johan Schröder,

Cand. philos.

La Crosse, Wis.
Trykt og forlagt af Forfatteren.
1867.

PART 2

Johan Schrøder

—❖—

The Scandinavians

in

the United States and Canada

with Reports and Information from

200 Scandinavian Settlements

_____

A Guide

for

Emigrants from the Old Country and for

the Settler in America

By

Johan Schrøder

Cand. Philos.

_____

La Crosse, Wis.

Printed and Published by the Author

1867

Introduction to "A Book for Scandinavians at Home and in America," in Emigranten, 1863

— ∴ —

For the Norwegian who sets out to leave the narrow valley of his fore-fathers it is difficult to know what is fact and what is pure invention in the many accounts of the New World that are pressed upon him.[1] It is therefore high time that something be done to help him to distinguish between truth and falsehood in matters that are of vital interest for the emigrant and his family.

At home the emigrant who seeks advice on where he should settle in America faces prejudice from all quarters. If he goes to the bookstore and demands guidebooks for these to-him-unknown territories, he will as a rule be given accounts published by public or private landowners and speculators who all praise the glories of their own land and recommend the cheapest and fastest route to these unequalled treasures. Should the emigrant wisely decide to disregard these biased and generally untruthful accounts, his only recourse is to seek information on the spot – in America. But on his arrival in Quebec he will soon discover that he has far too limited means to act independently and, consequently, that he again is forced to rely on the accounts and advice of others.

No truth-loving person can deny that for many years Quebec has been and still remains the worst den of robbers an emigrant may be trapped in. Early each spring the agents of railroads, steamship companies, and land speculators assemble here. In advance they have fought viciously among themselves, but now they come to co-operate in sharing the bounty. At sea the emigrant has observed the ability and authority of the ship's captain. He has learned to appreciate him and trust him, and will in most cases be inclined to follow his advice on how to travel farther west from Quebec. So agents and runners concentrate on the captain and seek by all means to bring him to their side. In nine of ten cases even the best of captains will be ensnared by them and, directly or indirectly, he is bribed to persuade the emigrants to buy tickets for one particular route. After much hustle and bustle the reloading is completed and the emigrant can continue on his westward journey. Along the way, however, land agents do their best to lure him to those lands they are commissioned to sell, and the emigrant will often interrupt his journey and acquire land far from his original destination. Not until he has gained experience and is able to evaluate his own situation does he realize that he has come to the wrong place and that he has lost time in labour that will yield less profit.

When a group of emigrants leave Quebec or another port the agent for the railroad or the shipping company will inform his headquarters by telegram about their expected arrival. But their representatives will often wait in vain and eventually discover that the emigrants will never arrive since they have been detoured by agents of competing companies and sent off by another route.

The emigrant will either have a definite place in mind where he will find family or friends, and then he will be well taken care of on arrival, or he is simply looking for suitable land. In the latter case he is again exposed to unnecessary expenses and runs the risk of making mistakes. In effect he cannot claim that his journey is at an end before he has found the spot where he will live and work. Since the northern states alone cover a greater area than many kingdoms in Europe, it may be appreciated that the emigrant cannot set out on endless travels in search of the best land. Simply by chance he may find an ideal place, but more often he finally stops from exhaustion and builds his home in a place that he would not have selected had he had more experience.

The point is, briefly, that even for the naturally gifted Scandinavian farmer, who has the intelligence and skill to arrive at his final destination without significant mishaps, there will have been so many unforeseen opportunities to make his wallet lighter that he will have suffered unnecessary losses on his way.

Cand. philos. Schrøder, who himself is a farmer, has left Norway in order to undertake the experiences of an emigrant. All summer he has been travelling throughout those parts of America that in the immediate future will be of the greatest interest for Scandinavian emigration. Canada has been traversed from one end to the other and Schrøder has penetrated the still-unsettled areas and examined the quality of the land. From Canada our fellow countryman came to the United States in August, and since then he has travelled mainly in Illinois and Iowa. From there he will continue to Wisconsin and Minnesota in order to study with his own eyes the facts of the emigrant's situation and circumstances.

The results of this tour will be published in America next year, and the book will be sold as cheaply as possible so that it can reach those for whom it is written, "the emigrant of few means and little income." The author will provide the book with a map. He, so to speak, takes the emigrant by his hand and says: "Come, let us travel on from Quebec or New York and try to reach our destinations the cheapest and best way possible. We may stop at any place and take a closer look at the land without much extra cost – if we don't behave foolishly. By studying the situation of those countrymen we meet on our way we may make some assumptions about how we may fare if we follow his example or avoid his mistakes."

The book will also be of use to Scandinavians who have already settled in America. There are, for instance, Scandinavians in Canada who because of biased or false accounts have such suspicion of the United States that they are happy that they are far removed from their miserable countrymen here. And vice versa, there are many Scandinavians in the United States who believe that happiness and freedom do not exist among farmers in Canada. All Scandinavians would surely have much to learn by reading the account of a man who does not travel as a paid agent and does not receive any kind of private or public subsidy on his journey. His observations present the situation as it is, without any bias. It may be that many a Scandinavian reader of this book will be led to reflect on his choice of settlement and consider moving to more fertile lands. But it may also be that the malcontent, who always sees the advantages in that which is at a distance but only the disadvantages in his own situation, may, by following Mr Schrøder from East to West, learn to appreciate his own home and decide that he is quite well off where he is and should hold on to what he has rather than seek a doubtful happiness somewhere else.

Mr Schrøder is, as we have already mentioned, a farmer himself and is therefore far better equipped than the average traveller to analyze the economic aspects of agriculture, but he intersperses economic and agricultural analyses with the narrative style of a tourist both in order to present his impressions as naturally as they appeared to him on his journey and in order to give the reader a pleasant change from descriptions of the land, which would otherwise be tiring if the only concern were forest and soil.

The author has called his book "American Diary," thus indicating that his unpretentious work has been written during his actual travels. If the emigrant follows the author's directions he will be able to liberate himself from the advice of runners and other dubious persons and continue his journey to any place in North America that a Scandinavian may benefit from visiting.

CHAPTER 1

Across the Atlantic

In the month of June 1863 I boarded the Norwegian steamship *Ganger Rolf*.[1] My first goal was Liverpool. From here I was to continue my journey by one of those steamship lines that weekly take passengers and freight across the ocean to Quebec in Canada. In Christiansand we received only a few more passengers but took in so much iced mackerel that the boxes filled the hold as well as the deck.[2] So we actually had fish as deck passengers. The small second-class cabin was extremely cold and damp because of all the boxes of ice that were stacked up against its thin walls. It was like being in an ice cellar day and night. If the crossing had taken several days I am sure we would have had illness on board. So we were all satisfied when we exchanged the smell of mackerel and the ice-cellar dampness of *Ganger Rolf* for the mild air of an English spring.

According to the Christiania agent for the English steamship company, I was to have a free steerage ticket from Liverpool, but the letters I had from him were of no avail. I was simply told that the promises and recommendations of a subagent were of no significance. Even my prior correspondence with the company, which was further evidence of the validity of my claims, was disregarded, and I had to accept the unforeseen expense of a ticket. The agent in Christiania was not to blame for my mistreatment. He had acted in good faith. Nor have I published this as a personal complaint but in order to make my countrymen aware of the fact that an agent's gilded promises and arrangements count for nothing. Once you have set out on your journey you are always more or less subject to the whims of your conveyors, and there is little use complaining or making trouble; indeed, such behaviour may even make matters worse. On board ship the crew and all servants are your masters. The mass of emigrants, who go by the lowest class, are treated as living cargo and must disperse or pack together according to the whims of the master. So it is best to enter the ship equipped with all the patience you can muster and remember that when the ship is on the open sea you will be treated according to the maxim "Now you are my pig." The company's agents in Hull and Liverpool received and dispatched the emigrants who had tickets for their line and it seemed to me that in particular the agent in Liverpool, a mulatto, fulfilled all the requirements that could be expected.

It is no easy matter to get your luggage through the purgatory of a British customs office. The far too large chests used by Norwegian emigrants – chests that require four men – make stevedores as well as crew that have to handle them impatient and surly, and as a consequence it is not unusual for the emigrant to discover that his chest has been broken or left behind. Often the emigrant will neglect to label his luggage properly as transit cargo for America via England and in such cases departure from Liverpool may be delayed by a whole week while the necessary papers that will satisfy British customs officers are procured. Through his own ignorance or negligence the emigrant can himself be responsible for the unexpected inconveniences that get in his way.

After two days in Liverpool we were taken by steam ferries out on the roadstead to the steamship the *Bohemian*.[3] Bowing and scraping, well-appointed servants guided the first-class passengers aft to the ship's gilded halls, while a few stewards with oilcloth caps on their heads and the mien of gaolers hurried the numerous steerage passengers down ladders to the bowels of the ship where there was hardly enough light for us to fight among ourselves for upper or lower berths, of which there were twenty in each cabin.

The next day we lay to at Londonderry in Ireland. Here we received several hundreds of the merry inhabitants of the island. They were in particularly high spirits because of the powerful effect of whiskey. On entering ship they were closely searched for their favourite liquor, and all compromising bottles were heaved overboard without further inspection of the degree of potency of their contents.[4] But the sons and daughters of Erin maintained their high spirits throughout the crossing, with or without whiskey, with or without hope of whiskey. The Irish, who were the last to arrive, were allotted the poorest quarters according to the accepted custom for emigrants from England, Scotland, and the rest of Europe area always considered to be better than the Irish.

We expected to see the coast of America after eight days at sea but these were eight long days, and nights as well. He who has lived in dirt and squalor at home will be helped to endure such a passage by the force of habit, and he who is used to better treatment will similarly be helped by his hope for early redemption. But when newspapers and pamphlets recommend second-class steamship passage to America as comfortable, I must lodge a protest. At least when I crossed the Atlantic, it was torture for most steerage passengers, even though we were favoured by exceptionally good weather. We all tried to sleep away as much time as possible, with the exception of the Irish, who were awake literally both night and day, dancing and merry-making by night, offering prayers of penance and promises of a new life by day. When we were given the orders to retire from the upper deck at nightfall most of us went to bed, but the Irish, females as well as males, along with about forty grey-clad boys who had graduated from an institution for the "morally depraved" as ripe for America[5] – all of these lined up to the sound of bagpipes for a kind of tramping dance. A monotonous din reached our stunned ears every time there was a general tramp, leading us to believe that the ship had received major damage.

Early every morning we were ordered out of bed and immediately stewards entered our cabins with plates of sulphur. These were placed on the floor and ignited to hasten the evacuation of the berths. When you realize that there was only room for six of us to dress at a time and that we were twenty in all in each cabin, you will appreciate that the whole team could be observed running pell-mell in their linen into the common mess room to escape suffocation from the sulphurous fumes. The commanding fumigator-in-chief would often come down to us with a group of first-class passengers to entertain them with the screams of women and children and the spectacle of general confusion during fumigation. Our cabin, however, was spared from this operation after the first occurrence when we notified the fumigator-in-chief that upon landing we would publish our complaints in the newspaper if he continued his experiments with our lungs. The twenty-year-old conceited Englishman responded with scorn and harsh words, but the head under-steward impressed him in our favour later that same day. For this steward was imbued with particular respect for some Australian gold-miners and myself because each of us had paid him 10 shillings for extra meals from the first-class dining-room. The next day I was summoned by the fumigator-in-chief, who presented himself as an experienced doctor who, as advertised, was responsible for the health of the passengers. He explained that the fumigation was performed to promote discipline as well as health, and admitted that the cure was unpleasant but that it was preferable to cleansing the air with red-hot irons dipped in tar, since that could easily cause a disastrous fire. He also added that he would pass our door by in the future.

Tables and benches that were slung from the ceiling of the common mess room were then taken down by the stewards and breakfast was served. The published breakfast menu consists of tea, sugar, coffee, or chocolate; fresh bread or wheat biscuit; and butter; but in fact what we got was brown water with a little sugar that was supposed to be coffee. I never saw any chocolate; the bread was passable but the biscuits were hard and dry and made of cornmeal. For my part I ate heartily at almost all meals and all passengers usually had enough to eat, but the published menu was nevertheless not adhered to.

After breakfast young and old went up to the upper deck to enjoy the fresh air and seek the limited entertainment available on board. The Irish nation would sit in long rows with pale faces after the deeds of night and whisper their prayers under the guidance of a Catholic priest. Now and then all would bow their heads at a given signal and then all lips would again begin to move silently. They could sit in this manner with expressionless faces for several hours at a time, and reminded us of a herd chewing the cud. The Irish prayer service, however, did not keep the other nationalities from practising their view of life. The Germans laid grand and loud-voiced plans for the future; an English brass band, whose unharmonious music had not been appreciated at home, were practising "Dixie" and other Yankee Doodles; bagpipers scared off all without Scottish blood in their veins to the other end of the deck; and children of all ages tumbled about everywhere. In all this hustle and bustle good spirits and friendliness prevailed. Nowhere either before or since have I seen so much disharmony find such harmonious expression.

It is soon time for dinner and the arrogant band of waiters – these water bees of the busy global hive – may be seen marching with roasts, pies, jellies, and puddings for the abundant table of the few first-class passengers. Any observer would realize that wages for all these servants and the cost of all this fine food could not have been covered by the tickets paid by the few first-class passengers. In fact, the steerage passengers pay for all this luxury: but on English steamers these are treated as pariahs and drummed down to their simple meal illuminated by the open hatchways through which draughts and cold air have access day and night.

Our dinner is also quite nice on paper, but I never saw other fare than either soup and salt beef (we were never given pork or bacon) or dried cod. It is not so much the fare itself that I object to but rather to the extremely nonchalant manner in which the ship's cooks were allowed to prepare it. Neither meat nor fish was soaked in advance but was thrown into the pot right from the salt barrel or the fish box. Consequently, the fish was almost inedible. All this salt food every day led to constant thirst and an enormous consumption of water. I do not mention all this as a complaint but as a warning to other emigrants. The health of the emigrant on arrival is not at all inconsequential, for as soon as he sets foot in America he is faced with trials the outcome of which depends entirely on his own resourcefulness. It would have been a simple matter for the cooks to accommodate the modest wishes of the steerage passengers, but we will wait in vain for any improvement on British ships in this respect. For the ship-owners have the ingrained prejudice that a real gentleman goes first class and that there is no reason to fear the grumblings of the poor people in steerage. Consequently, the former are provided with luxurious food, service, and quarters, for which the company is publicly awarded with praise and fame, while the latter are not even given food they can digest or a place where they can lie down protected from draughts and colds. On top of all this is the insolence of the waiters. They turned deaf ears to complaints and entreaties and I saw with my own eyes that they would jokingly throw the tinware of the poor emigrants overboard pretending that it was in their way. The loss of these utensils was especially severe here where all were jealous of their own interests. The ship's captain never condescended to recognize the steerage passengers, and the crew, a half-disciplined riff-raff from all corners of the world, were rude and repulsive, except when engaging the emigrants' assistance in the heaviest hauls when hawsers or sails needed adjustment.

The afternoon would pass in much the same way as the morning. The Irish prayed and slept and the passengers would often stand in front of the blackboard where the daily progress of the ship was noted.

Supper was much like breakfast. The weak and the ill would have preferred the gruel promised in the advertised menu, but it was available only once or twice during the crossing and then not in sufficient quantities. Half of the applicants were turned down when they held up their tin cups to the distributor of soup. During meals the mess hall looked like a pigsty, but what else could be expected when five-six hundred people were thronged together in a limited space and were weaving in and out to get their rations of soup, tea, butter, potatoes, et cetera. In the process considerable portions of soup and butter left their traces on nearby coats and jackets. In addition, you should try to imagine the uninhibited disgorging of the seasick before the eyes of the diners, and you may have some notion of the delights of the table in steerage. I would recommend that emigrants bring some canned meat or fowl, purchased in advance, that they may enjoy in their own cabin. If they should have some tins left after the crossing, they can sell them at twice the original price here in America, where game fowl is an unknown food except in the West, where there are wild pigeons and prairie hens.

A couple of the larger cabins were marked "Hospital." The sick, however, were never permitted to enter this section since our steward had occupied it for his trade in *porter* and *ale*.[6] Whenever he blinked his left eye at the gold-miners and myself, we knew that the message was: "Go to the hospital. The cook has brought me some delicacies from the first class." So we, who were among the healthiest on board, made up the hospital's patients, while those who were really ill had to stay in their narrow berths. No kind of medicine was ever dispensed to the ill: The ship's doctor appeared only in his office as fumigator. Suffocating fumes of sulphur seemed to be his universal cure and he lavished it upon all.

At nightfall the deck was cleared, lamps were lighted in the hold, and all went to rest, except for the Irish and the London youths who were waiting for the bagpipes to call them to dance. Such were the daily routines except for Sundays, which were distinguished by a sermon held in the first-class cabin and plum pudding served in the steerage. All were permitted to hear the sermon. In the beautifully appointed lounge our old aquaintance the ship's doctor, alias the fumigator-in-chief, performed in the role of clergyman, reading from a book of homilies a sermon on the text for the day as well as the appropriate prayers. Considering his behaviour towards the passengers in the forward part of the ship, it would have been more in keeping with the holy office to have given this duty to another of the ship's officers. It should be forgiven that many an eye wandered from object to object in the lounge. Above the table, the entire length of the lounge, were shelves from which bottles of Madeira and port sparkled. If the doctor had noticed the many pale and weak men and women who had staggered on tottering legs to the far corners of the room, if he had but had a spark of the love that he hypocritically recommended to his listeners, then he would have poured a glass of Madeira or port for the weak and suffering, and that would have been far more beneficial than religious sentiments from lips such as his.

One beautiful morning we were told that by evening we could expect to reach and pass Newfoundland. What happiness could now be observed on all faces. All days the bow was crowded with groups of emigrants who looked for the first distant view of the cliffs of Newfoundland. When towards evening we sailed along the coast of the island to get to its southern point, Cape Race, the crew began talking about the wreck of the line's emigrant ship the *Anglo Saxon* a few months earlier. The ship ran on some rocks in a snowstorm, was lost, and most of the passengers and crew lost their lives.[7] In autumn, spring, and winter these waters at the entrance to the St Lawrence and Quebec are dangerous to navigate because of the heavy fog that can lie here for weeks at a time.

We were soon to experience that fog can be a serious matter in the latter part of June as well. At Cape Race we were met by a boat that brought American news and took back news from Europe.[8]

"What is new?" asked our captain.

"Bad news," was the reply. "The company's best emigrant steamer, the *Norwegian*, has gone down someplace between here and Quebec. Five hundred passengers are supposed to have landed on some rocky island and you, Captain, have been ordered to find the shipwrecked and bring them into Quebec."[9]

The *Norwegian* had departed from Liverpool eight days before our ship and was never to return again. Our captain had to change his course, and our features fell somewhat at the news of this interruption of our journey. But soon we were all interested observers of the steps that were taken on board to locate the shipwreck and the preparations to rescue the survivors. The hatches below the steerage deck were opened and the ship's catacombs soon echoed with activity and the blows of hammers. On the upper deck cannon were loaded and rockets were mounted. The first night we sailed a south-easterly course towards the coast of Nova Scotia. Every now and then a rocket was fired, but without any response. The next day we sailed north along the Cape Breton Islands. Nowhere had the wrecked steamship or its crew and passengers been seen. When dark fell again we began to fire our cannon and rockets without cease. It was a beautiful sight, not easily forgotten by me or my fellow passengers, to see the blue, red, and yellow rockets flare in the sky and linger there long after the ship had passed them by. It was past midnight and still the passengers could not be persuaded to go to bed. Indeed, the beautiful fireworks in the calm night so preoccupied us that for a while we forgot its purpose – until distant cannon fire to the north made us look in that direction. Our ship responded with a powerful cannonade and after a while we could see a flame in the sky from a point many miles distant. We had arrived at the goal of our search, but the captain did not dare to approach the rockbound island of St Paul in the dark because of the breakers. Therefore he manoeuvred back and forth until the first break of day, when all boats were set down to go to land.

The unfortunate captain of the *Norwegian* came aboard with the first boatload. He explained that he had gone at half-speed for two days and nights because of the fog. Finally he was sure that he had passed the dangerous St Paul and went full throttle. After sailing for a few hours through fog that was so thick he could not see his own hand, the great ship grounded with such an impact on a sloping rock that the bow was raised twelve feet higher than the stern. The ship then heeled towards the rocks so that all on deck – it was now nine o'clock in the morning – partly fell down on the rocks and partly lowered themselves on ropes. The mighty ship of iron had not moved since but when I saw it the stern was below the surface. All passengers were saved, and the crew, who were no angels, had salvaged whatever they had found suitable for their own use. In other words, all discipline had ceased and in the confusion the seamen had stolen and robbed whatever they could carry off and hidden it among the rocks. The comic is often mixed with the tragic. Thus one of the English passengers had laughed when he observed one of the sailors making off with a small but heavy box he had brought with him from England. The sailor thought he had discovered the Englishman's store of gold, while the box merely contained lead and shells for a hunting expedition in Canada.

After stumbling and crawling for many hours in the fog over the jagged and steep rocks, the shipwrecked finally came to a small incline where there was enough level ground for a camp. They had neither roof nor firewood. When the fog cleared away the captain returned to the ship with some of his reliable crew and brought back boats, sails, and provisions. Of the sails they made tents, while masts and other woodwork were cut for firewood. An American cutter approached the next day and offered help but the captain, who was well aware of the nature of such assistance, distributed the ship's arms among the passengers and let the Yankees know that they would receive a warm welcome should they dare to approach. Every night the shipwrecked fired a salvaged cannon and lighted a fire to make other ships aware of their predicament. After having waited in vain for eight days, many were despondent when help finally arrived. It was indeed good luck that all lives were saved when all could easily have been lost in the waves. Had the ship hit a cliff rather than a beach, it would have gone right down and only the best swimmers would have had a chance of reaching land.[10]

With a double load of passengers and crew our ship now continued its journey to Quebec. The once-proud *Norwegian* was beyond salvaging and would disappear completely with the first heavy onshore wind. I was told that the company had lost six good steamships in as many years, all wrecked in the fog off this section of the American coast. On a later crossing, in the fall of that same year, the very ship I had travelled on was lost and several people were drowned in these same waters. This should be sufficient warning of the risk run by immigrants who in spring or fall board steamships that will pass through the fog belt of Newfoundland on their way to Quebec.

When we reached the mouth of the St Lawrence River between the low, swampy island of Anticosti and, for Norwegians, the ill-famed

Gaspé[11] on the south bank of the river, we still had four hundred miles to go to Quebec. Had New York been our goal, we would have completed our journey by this time. The passage up the St Lawrence prolongs the journey by four hundred miles. From morning till night all eyes were set upon the coasts of Gaspé, Témiscouata, and Kamouraska as we sailed past them. The white-painted houses on the bank seemed inviting and the frequent columns of smoke that rose to the skies from the spruce forests were witness to the hard work of the settlers' axes. It was of course impossible to evaluate the quality of the soil simply by sailing past the landscape, and yet this has often been done by authors who in fact have seen America only from the railroad and the steamship. Although we wrote 21 June, the air was keen as in spring in Norway's interior regions. All the way to Quebec the grass seemed hardly tall enough for grazing. The cold winds from Greenland and the damp ocean fog stunt the vegetation, even though there should be sufficient sunlight here at forty-eight degrees north latitude. Farther west, where mountains and forests form barriers to the polar winds, conditions are far better. On 22 June, ten days out from Liverpool, the *Bohemian* arrived at Quebec, the largest port of Lower Canada and England's Gibraltar in North America.

The release of the large mass of emigrant baggage took a surprisingly short time. The steam-lifts on board worked so fast that all boxes, chests, suitcases, and bags were on the wharf shortly after noon as the owners, most of them with anxious expressions on their faces because of the novelty of their situation, held on to the few possessions that they had salvaged from their former fatherland and that now were to help them in laying a foundation for their future in their new one.

At this point in my narrative I would like to consider the advantages and disadvantages of the two kinds of emigrant conveyance across the Atlantic: steam and sail.[12] For the emigrant family but little used to the sea, either alternative will to some extent be a torture. If such a family counts several members unfit for work, a sailing ship is recommended since the ticket for a steamship may cost up to 45 specie-dalers,[13] and this money may be better used for the purchase of land. It should count as no great advantage for the head of the family that his dependents can boast of having crossed the ocean in ten days rather than six weeks. On sailing ships fitted out by Scandinavian owners the emigrants receive far better treatment from captain and crew than on the steamships of other nations. Our own seamen are more disciplined than the English and the Americans and they also have too much charity to treat the emigrant as an unfeeling piece of baggage. If wrongs should be committed on Scandinavian ships, retribution would be exacted upon their owners and their officers since the Scandinavian press in North America is now so powerful that complaints will also be broadcast in Scandinavia.

All this is different on the great steamers. On these, officers as well as crew have developed the art of doing the least work for the most pay. Heartless stewards keep the helpless emigrants at arm's length or treat them unfairly. Complaints do not reach the ears of the owners or if they do they are not noticed as long as the ships are filled with passengers and make good money. Single people who can count on finding work on arrival in America should nevertheless chose steam since the shorter passage deprives them of fewer workdays. Going by steam saves an average of thirty days, and in this time a hire of $1.50 a day will be ample remuneration for the ticket. But I would definitely warn against going to Quebec by steamship in the spring or the fall. In these seasons the lines to New York are far safer. Not a single steamer is lost going to New York in the time it takes to lose five going to Quebec. Railroad tickets to the northwestern United States cost the same from both ports. That some individuals may have found steerage passage to their liking does not affect the main points in my description, where I have not paid so much attention to how I myself fared there as I have to the plight of the large host of poor, helpless emigrant families who always make up the majority of those who travel by the lowest class.

CHAPTER 2

Canada East or Lower Canada

All the emigrants who planned to continue farther west and who had sufficient funds prepared themselves for the journey on Canada's great Grand Trunk Railway.[1] By five o'clock that same afternoon all was ready for their continued journey. After all the anxiety and excitement they had been exposed to in the course of this their first day, with the arrangement of their baggage and the purchasing of tickets, I considered them lucky when they had settled in their seats on the train. The emigrant, however, must never for a moment forget that he is on foreign soil, whether he be in England or in America. Many an innocent Norwegian, who desires to begin his observations as soon as possible, will regret sticking his head out the window as the train begins to move. Before he is aware that anything is happening, his head-dress has disappeared. Nimble-fingered thieves are on the spot and expertly remove hats and caps from heads at the windows, to teach the foreigners, as they explain, to salute America politely. Grip, a cobbler from Bergen, and some farmers from Østerdal were in this manner relieved of their Pennsylvania fur winter caps upon leaving Quebec in the fall of 1866.[2] Thieves are on hand as soon as the train begins to move and there is no longer any danger of being pursued.

Since I had determined to make myself acquainted with the Canadian landscape and its agricultural possibilities, I remained in Quebec in order to acquire the necessary supplies for excursions into the interior. In a later chapter I will return to the westward transportation available to the emigrant[3] and will now proceed to describe my travels in Canada and give my impression of the country.

Canada is divided into Canada East, or Lower Canada, and Canada West, or Upper Canada. The history of the country is, briefly told, as follows:

Columbus discovered the new continent, as all will know, in 1492. After this discovery there was a growing interest in further voyages

of discovery among several of the seagoing nations of Europe. In 1497
Henry VII of England sent Sebastian Cabot out to search for unknown
lands and he was the first seaman to reach the mainland of America.
He landed on the peninsula of Nova Scotia and is also said to have
entered the Gulf of St Lawrence. However that may be, it is certain
that Jacques Cartier, a famous navigator employed by the King of
France, discovered Canada in 1535. He landed in Quebec, or
Stadacona, as the natives called the place. Canada belonged to France
from 1535 to 1629, when Admiral Kirke took Quebec during the war
between England and France. This event, however, was of little significance since Canada was returned to France three years later. In 1759,
when these two powers again were at war with each other, General
Wolfe defeated the French troops defending Quebec and thereby took
not only the city but the whole country. Both Montcalm, the French
general, and Wolfe lost their lives in this battle, and the citizens of
Quebec raised a monument to both of them which visitors to Quebec
should see. The fall of Quebec marked the end of French rule in
Canada and in the peace treaty of 1763 the land was awarded to Great
Britain and the two countries have been united since that time.[4]

The size of Canada may be illustrated by the fact that it is three times
as large as all of Norway. Lower Canada is situated between forty-five
and forty-nine degrees north latitude; Upper Canada goes all the way
down to forty-two degrees north latitude, which is almost as far south
as Chicago in the United States.[5] In the east, Canada begins with the
coast of Labrador and in the west it stretches almost to the upper end
of Lake Superior. The land farther west also belongs to the British
crown but it is not considered part of Canada. In the north, Canada
borders on the Hudson Bay Territory and in the south on the Great
Lakes, The St Lawrence River, and the United States. Canada is about
seventeen hundred miles long and two hundred and fifty miles wide.

Canada was called the Province of Quebec until 1791, when it was
decided that the country was too large and sparsely populated for a
centralized government. Consequently, it was divided into the two
parts named above. In 1840, however, they were united under one
governor and a common Parliament. The population of Lower Canada
is mainly French while the English dominate Upper Canada.

Lower Canada extends on both sides of the St Lawrence River. I
decided to go by steamer to Montreal, a city farther up the river, and
from there to make excursions to the country south of the St Lawrence.
Since Quebec is so decidedly not the place for emigrants to linger,
a description of this city or of the other cities of America is outside
the scope of this book. The steamer to Montreal was filled with passengers and merry-making. For the first time I saw a large group of

lumberjacks and rafters who had come to Quebec with some large lumber rafts and who now were on their way back to the forests. Since they had been paid their wages in Quebec there is no need to explain that they were free with the shilling as well as the dollar and placed their money on the bar as long as they could take in whiskey and ale.[6] The foredeck was packed with ropes and canoes (scooped-out logs) that would be used again for the next rafting. Each time we met rafts floating down the river, the crews on them as well as their joyous comrades on our ship let off the well-known forest yell of America in lieu of our Norwegian hurrah. Since the rafts could have a crew of up to one hundred and we had at least a couple of hundred on board, you may imagine that we could be heard from afar as we proceeded up the river.

Among this bacchantic crowd two genuine sons of the forest could be observed moving calmly about – the first Indians I had seen: a father and his sixteen-year-old son returning from a winter hunting expedition that had taken them several hundred miles from home. Their large but light canoe, which was entirely made of birch-bark, was slung from the cabin ceiling. When the father – his name was John Watso – told me that he would leave the boat at Sorel, a town sixty miles from Montreal, and continue his journey home by canoe, I expressed my great desire to go with him to the village of his tribe. He did not give me any answer to my request, but just before midnight I felt someone touching my shoulder. It was the Indian, who asked me if I really had decided to follow him home, and on my "yes" he asked me to get ready right away since we would be in Sorel in a few minutes. Anyone who has read Cooper's narratives of America's native population must have acquired an interest in this proud race whom all refer to as "savages." I congratulated myself on this unexpected meeting. Only a few days back I had walked on the cobblestones of Christiania and now I was about to venture out in the pitch-black night on the frailest vessel ever devised and follow wild Indians to their remote retreat.

In Quebec I had learned that no reliable information on the land and its agricultural possibilities could be had from the agents of the government or the land companies. Each of them was cooking his own pot, each spoke only with a view to benefitting his employer or himself. I would have to see the land and its inhabitants for myself and become acquainted with all classes who earned their bread by the sweat on their brow, so that my book would be, not the product of a salaried pamphleteer, but a true account of Canadian conditions based on my own observations. Consequently, I eagerly grasped any opportunity to achieve this aim. Even though this often exposed me to hard toil and danger, I should explain that at this time I was under no obligation to be careful of my own person. I could sing, as could so many others,

I care for nobody, no! not I;
For nobody cares for me.[7]

The two Indians took their canoe on their shoulders, launched it on the river, and loaded it with their skins, sacks of dried venison, fox traps, and other equipment. For me they prepared a seat of skins in the middle of the canoe. When we had left the bank, the old man gave me something he asked me to take care of. I could not see it in the dark, but I realized he had given me their guns as a pledge of my own safety. We glided silently on Lake St-Pierre in the dark night. The Indians sat in either end of the canoe, making diligent use of their small paddles, and our pleasant conversation was interrupted only now and then by the cries of innumerable bullfrogs, which at times were so loud that they sounded as if a distant steamship had let out steam. I had to tell the Indians about Norway and the people I belonged to and in return the elder Indian answered all my questions about his tribe. At sunrise we arrived at their village a good journey up the St-François River.[8] News of our arrival spread quickly and the home of Watso received many visitors who wanted to see the results of his winter hunt. One of the sacks of dried venison was opened and tested. Each one tore off a small piece and ate it raw.

The village was well organized. Each small wood cabin had a field where corn and potatoes were cultivated. A typical house, with an attic and panelled rooms, cost about 400 Canadian silver dollars. The Indians walked around all day or did indoor chores. The hard work in the fields was done by French men and women hired for 25 cents a day and board. The Indian women on the other hand had more than enough work to do. Some worked on the seams of canoes, and a canoe that was large enough to hold ten men cost $15. Others sewed moccasins and gloves of deerskin that their men had cured solely with soap and oil. Thus each day passes with its own pleasures and troubles through the whole summer until the month of October, but then the village awakes to new life. It is time for hunting and all men who can follow the wolf and the deer or set a trap for fox, otter, and muskrat prepare for expeditions from which they will not return until spring.[9] The red man's hunting grounds diminish year by year and the various tribes have difficulty maintaining their population, even in Canada, where the government provides more than nominal support. In this the histories of all tribes are similar – if you have heard of one, you know the story of them all.

The sixty-four-year-old shaman of the Abnaki tribe, Peter Paul Osunkhirhine, told me that his people had first lived in and around Quebec.[10] When the French arrived, this led to continuous conflict with the white men and the outcome was that about a hundred and fifty years ago the tribe moved to the St-François River, where it selected a reservation of ten thousand acres of sandy soil.[11] When Watso was a youth, his great-grandmother died at a hundred and one years of age; she had told him that the tribe had first moved to an island farther downstream but that it was ravaged by diseases and the Abnakis decided to move to higher ground. The emigrant should not consider settling where even the hardy Indians cannot survive. Therefore we may give as a general rule that the immigrant should avoid the low and damp banks of rivers, however tempting the soil may seem for agriculture or livestock. The climate fever (the so-called *"ague and fever"*)[12] will surely get to him and break down his health and ruin his property.

In 1812 the tribe took part in England's war with the United States and the old Osunkhirhine wore an honourable but not very becoming scar across his nose in memory of his adventures.[13] The tribe suffered many losses in that war, but has since remained stable. There are now four hundred people in the village.[14] Each year some youths marry outside the tribe and are then no longer considered members. Such extra-tribal unions are not favoured but when they occur, the rule is that the man must forever leave his father and mother and belong to the tribe of his wife. But all Canadian tribes are bound together in friendship. The ancient tradition of renewing treaties and pacts every sixth year is still followed. The Mohawks, however, are an exception and they are regarded as the enemy by the Abnaki. The Mohawks still own a stretch of land close to Montreal. If one tribe is attacked by the whites, the others are bound to come to their assistance.

Watso's brother Joseph, the most striking Indian I have ever seen, said there were about four thousand Indian warriors in Canada. I asked them why they did not elect a common government so that the complaints of each tribe would have more weight with the Canadian government. Joseph thought that traditional rivalries and tribal pride made such a development impossible. The Indians have been made wards of the government. If an Indian's rights are threatened or he is otherwise mistreated by the whites he can not seek recourse in the courts on his own but must be represented by his guardian, the government. The Abnaki tribe is currently involved in a legal suit with the French concerning a stretch of land. Many members of the tribe speak both French and English. Indeed, the French language has gained considerable ground among the Indians all over the north-west; they have a greater liking for this language than for English, and the chances for a friendly response are greater if the visitor addresses them in French. The reason is that then they are sure that you are not a Yankee, a race they always fear, hate, or despise.

After sundown at midsummer here at forty-six degrees north latitude there is only a half-hour's dusk.[15] Throughout the village watch-fires were lighted outside each cabin and both sexes enjoyed themselves around the fires with conversation and all kinds of merriment. Stories in their own language, which were of no benefit to me, called forth smiles and even laughter from the grave reddish-brown faces with pipes in mouth. Many of the young people, however, were entertaining themselves by running about and wrestling virtually in the nude. The aim was to press your adversary towards the fire and each time one of them succeeded, whether through skill or sheer strength, the victor was greeted with the Indian forest yell. Others wandered around making practical jokes. There were, for instance, three young Indians with *stove-pipes*[16] (top hats) on their heads and lighted cigars in their mouths, but otherwise *in puris naturalibus*,[17] who came sauntering towards us in an exaggeratedly dandified manner. They were pretending to be Yankees and as they passed the fire we were sitting at, one of them exclaimed haughtily, *"All Indians, I guess."* A young girl picked up a brand from the fire to "Teach the Yankees manners," as she put it, but she was turned away with: *"Get away, you squaw,"* which together with the general laughter at the procession embarrassed her so much that she retired.[18] It was all in fun, but these and other episodes nevertheless demonstrated how well these intelligent Indians understand and are sensitive to the attitudes and prejudices of most white people. The fire died out under the majestic elms that overshadowed the village and I went with the others to my bed of deerskins and to a good night's sleep after a day-long waking dream.

The truly comfortable days that I passed with this tribe I owe mainly to Joseph Watso, an Indian of great physical strength who was also exceptionally intelligent and a gentleman to boot. On one of our walks we came to an establishment owned by a Frenchman, and I ordered two glasses of cognac. The servant poured one glass only as he rudely remarked that the "savage" could not be served any liquor. Joseph grew angry immediately, but he quickly gained control of himself and smiled: "No, give me a glass of water." I was still too young in America to realize the privileges of skin, and it was annoying to witness the haughty manner in which a pompous but insignificant clerk dared to address a man who had been tried in hardship and danger. Out of respect for the offended Indian I also refused refreshments. On his long journeys Joseph had several times come across Norwegians living alone in the forest far from any settlement. He had noted their exceptional strength and the endurance they demonstrated in carrying provisions from the traders to their homes.

When I parted from these friendly people they insisted that I return for their major celebration in October, when the whole tribe would gather before the hunters set out on their winter expeditions. I really would have liked to be able to accept that offer, but when they also, and not merely in jest, offered me one of the young girls of the tribe as a wife and asked me to settle among them, I gave the confirmed bachelor's well-known answer.

After the recent Indian war in Minnesota there has been a widespread fear of the red man.[19] In Europe the presence of the Indians is used as a scarecrow to stop emigration, and a large number of Americans are also more or less afraid of them. The confrontations I have described here, as well as those I experienced later, have taught me that when the European approaches the Indians openly and deals with them as his equals in all and everything, he will have nothing to fear, at least in a country where neither government nor private corporations have deliberately tried to cheat, subdue, or debase them. The Canadian government has in this respect stood up to its duty. It has not entered into deceptive treaties with the red men and it has so consistently restrained the white population from exercising their avarice on the Indians that there now exists a tacit feeling of reciprocal sympathy between the two races. The areas that the Indians have been awarded cannot be taken from them on any pretext.

The relationship between the races is different in the United States, where the government is merely an expression of the often-unprincipled shifts in popular desires. There, the Indian has so frequently been the victim of large-scale deceits that he has lost all faith in the white man. Consequently, the pioneer can never safely settle in their vicinity since he will risk reaping the consequences of the fraudulent dealings of office-holders, of whom the emigrant is ignorant, who makes fortunes at the Indians' expense.

The rural population was without exception French, but frequently mixed with Indian blood. Both men and women were small of stature and seemed unhealthy. There were often black shadows below the eyes of the women and both sexes had the appearance of belonging to a race that has outlived its time. French was the only language spoken and there was little sympathy for the English.

The air was warm and humid, probably above twenty degrees Réaumur[20] in the latter part of June wherever the land was protected from the cold winds from the sea. On my return to Sorel I discovered a small fleet of canoes loaded with the produce of the land: eggs, chickens, ducks, fish, vegetables, cheese, and butter. Eels thick as a man's arm were sold for 12 cents each. The small quantities of produce brought by each farmer suggested that the cultivated areas of the farms were small.

At the hotel in Sorel I again met with the Indian shaman. At table a trinket pedlar discovered him and clung to him like a leech trying to get him to buy rings, ear-rings, and the like from his collection of baubles. Finally he even offered him his whole casket to take home to his tribe so that they might select what they wanted while he would wait in Sorel until the Indian returned. But the old Indian remained unperturbed. Later on I asked the pedlar whether he knew the Indian. No, he didn't, but he had always found the Indians to be honest and never hesitated to give them credit or to let them have his wares for inspection. When I told him that he had been trying to tempt the shaman of the tribe he gaped: That was the worst customer he could have wasted time and effort on.

I arrived in Montreal equipped with a recommendation from the chief emigration agent for Canada, Mr Buchanan,[21] to the administration of the Grand Trunk Railway. After a day of running back and forth I finally met the superintendent, Mr Brydges,[22] just as he was about to depart for New York. On the pier he made a few notes on my document and these scribblings proved to be worth a general pass for all travel on the Grand Trunk, a stretch of fourteen hundred miles, from that date to 30 September. This valuable assistance relieved me of all troubles and Canada was now open to me.

In Montreal I looked up the Norwegians then living there. Captain Gjertsen from Tromsø, who was loading wheat, kindly invited me to partake of the hospitality of his comfortable cabin.[23] The mechanic Guthus, who was employed as a tinsmith at $40 in silver a month, showed me the kindness of accompanying me on my visits to several Norwegians. Bekkelund, a saddler, had a good income as an upholsterer. The few Norwegians who live here feel rather abandoned since they are so few and thus have a strong inclination to move on to join their countrymen, who have settled in such large numbers in the United States. A wagonsmith from Drammen, Haugan, was also living here at the moment and he is recognized by the Norwegians as an emigration agent.[24] As such he was sent to Norway and persuaded the majority of the group he brought back with him to settle in Canada. He was fully convinced that he had made the best choice for his countrymen and had himself bought three hundred acres of forest land in the so-called "Eastern Townships." After building a house and clearing forty acres, he left it all in 1862 because he saw no future for himself and his large family as a farmer. In Montreal he and one of his sons work in a brewery for 75 cents each per day. When I later visited the area where he had farmed I was able to form my own opinion concerning the judgment so quickly passed by popular opinion on Norwegian emigration agents.[25]

CHAPTER 3

Lower Canada South of the St Lawrence River

From this day, the first of July, my real study of Canada began. My journey went from west to east and north-east, covering the area south of the main artery of Canada, the St Lawrence River. After we had passed the famous stone bridge across the St Lawrence[1] we came to a wide stretch of sand that extended all the way to the Richelieu River. All this land had been cultivated since the earliest times. The soil consisted entirely of sand and the fields had a poor growth. The land was free of stumps and the field strips were about four yards wide. There was little meadow and there were relatively few cattle, considering the size of the farms. All this suggests that the soil has been exhausted. Indeed, without rain at the right times it is difficult to get a profitable harvest. Since most of the land is owned by seigniories (estates from the time the French crown owned the land and gave it away or sold it) and the farmers are tenants, they have little interest in doing much for the long-term improvement of the soil. The emigrant will probably not want to be a tenant when he can acquire cheap land for himself. Consequently, I will not go into details concerning tenant farming. The emigrant with capital, however, could acquire for himself the influence and life-style of the titled aristocracy of Europe by purchasing a seigniory.[2]

Farther east, from the Richelieu to the Yamaska River, the sandy soil contained more clay and the fields therefore had a better appearance. All the land is owned by seigniories. Still farther east, between the Yamaska and the St-François rivers, there were large stretches of forest that had been devastated by fire and were only fit for firewood. In the frequent clearings the stumps were left standing everywhere. The soil had obviously not been cultivated for more than ten to twelve years. Ridding the land of all stumps would have cost about $40 in silver per acre. This improvement of the soil is therefore seldom seen in America; indeed, it is scoffed at because of the expenses involved.

One simply leaves the stumps to the ravages of time, and it takes fifteen or more years before this last vestige of the primeval forest and main barrier to efficient farming has disappeared. During the first years the succession of crops is generally as follows: buckwheat for the first two years, oats in the third; the fourth year fertilizer is used sparingly and wheat or barley is sowed in this and the fifth year. Only in the sixth year should one attempt to cultivate a meadow without fertilizing it. In Norway, cultivated meadow is not found profitable if it has not been fertilized from the start, but this rule does not seem to apply anywhere in America. Even on mediocre land the soil has first been exhausted with successive harvests before grass is sown in the exhausted and weedy soil. Along the rivers the soil is usually sandy; farther up there is forest, but only infrequently is there clay soil.

The Eastern Townships, where the best land Lower Canada has to offer the pioneer farmer is to be found, begin on the west bank of the St-François River, about seventy miles east of Montreal.[3] I remained a few days in and around the beautiful town of Richmond, on the west bank of the river. In the immediate vicinity the asking price for a hundred-acre property, with about fifty acres of it cultivated and partly cleared of stumps, is from $1,300 to $2,000 in silver. In this part of the country good pasturage can not be counted on till the end of May, and towards the end of October cattle are taken in for the winter. Wheat is paid $4.00 for four bushels and $3.00 for the same amount of barley. On a farm where eighty acres were actually cultivated I discovered that the average complement of livestock was about twenty head of cattle, four horses, and twenty-five sheep. Each year on this farm thirty acres are used for crops, thirty acres are for hay, and twenty are used for pasture. For a loan with a first-priority mortgage in this farm the owner paid 7 per cent. The government follows the rule of selling all timber on crown property before land is sold to the emigrant. The public coffers benefit from this, but the emigrant loses because he is thereby denied the possibility of paying for his land with the timber. Since it is still usual to leave all timber with less than fourteen-inch tops standing, there is still plenty of timber for building purposes as well as firewood for the settler. In Richmond I visited Jacobsen, a shoemaker from Fredrikshald.[4] He had worked at his trade here for three years and was able to set aside about $200 each year. A carpenter named Saxlund also lived and worked here. Times were difficult, he said. He made $1.50 a day and board. On walking around, I discovered that Englishmen and Americans were invariably in possession of farms from one hundred to three hundred acres while the French were satisfied with fifty acres. The former think of their children's future, the latter only of themselves.

From friendly Richmond I journeyed on for twenty-five miles along the St-François River in a south-easterly direction to the lumber and mill town of Sherbrooke in search of the main agent for all Company land for sale in the Eastern Townships.[5] The road passed through a gently waving landscape with woods in the background, but all the nasty-looking stump fields in the foreground often interrupted the beautiful scene. The air is pure and good for breathing, but it is altogether lacking in that freshness that the nightly northern breezes from the mountains give to the summer air of Norway.[6] More than a beautiful landscape and atmospheric balsam, however, are needed to inspire the local population. Crass materialism on the one side and absurd religious fanaticism on the other turned people's heads.[7] Traces of copper had been found here and there and the area swarmed with men in search of copper who dreamed of leading both the rich capitalist and the poor worker out of Stone Age conditions into the semi-Golden Age of copper. Many farmers were more concerned with their legal rights to the copper that was yet to be found on their land than with the potatoes that were verifiably there. Indeed, there were instances of farmers who had turned down offers of several thousands for land that was scarcely worth more than a few hundred.[8]

While most of the population were in this manner dreaming of sudden wealth, a small but faithful flock in Richmond were gathered around a preacher from Boston who had just arrived there with the intention of being taken with his congregation alive into heaven direct from Richmond on a specified day. However incredible it may seem, many of the faithful had actually given away their possessions indiscriminately, to family as well as to strangers, so that nothing of this world should weigh them down during the ascension. On the pre-determined day the congregation were gathered around their fanatic preacher in their church, singing hymns from morning till night, waiting for the roof to open and the miracle to proceed. Hundreds of curious onlookers stood outside the church, wanting to see how it all would end. When the sun had set and the congregation was beginning to realize they had been fooled, the preacher found fit to announce that the Lord had just revealed to him that the day of ascension was postponed because of their sinful ways. The crestfallen conned returned to their empty homes while the con-man's agile assistant led him through the crowd and into the forest before anyone could have a word with him.

The authorities take steps to encourage non-Catholics to settle in these townships in order to lessen the dominance of the Catholic French. Therefore the gates are thrown wide for the worst kinds of religious leaders, sectarian lay preachers who must be shunned – in particular by the Scandinavian settlers who have no ministers of their own in Canada – not only for their peace of mind and peace within their families but for success in their endeavours. In my conversations with Mr Hennechau,[9] the main Company agent in this part of the country, I stressed the necessity of a government initiative for bringing in Scandinavian Lutheran ministers if a Scandinavian settlement was to succeed. After a few years interest in their own improved land would tie the settlers to the area, but the lack of ministers and parochial schools would eventually be so strongly felt that they would depart, even at a great loss, and head for the United States, where their brethren in the North-west have organized congregations with churches as well as schools. The authorities would have to pay the ministers' salaries, at least for the first three years, and the government or the Land Company would have to provide the settlement with a parsonage. The agent fully agreed, but as far as I know nothing has been done and Canada cannot boast a single successful Norwegian, Swedish, or Danish settlement.

On the agent's request I went to visit a poor Norwegian woman who had been left behind by her family. She now lived in Sherbrooke, where the English inhabitants took such good care of her that she had no great desire to leave the place. Her name was Anne Andersdatter Skeie and she was from the parish of Eiken some miles north of Farsund.[10] She had arrived in America in 1860 with her son, Søren, and daughter-in-law. In 1862 her son and his wife left her and have not been heard from since.

I declined Mr Hennechau's offer of employment as emigration agent in the service of his company. However, I gratefully accepted his letters of introduction to the Norwegian Tambs and the company agents Pennoyer and Farwell, all in the town of Bury in Compton County, where a group of Norwegian settlers had lived for several years.[11]

The heavy stage-coach pulled by three horses, two on either side of the shaft and one up front, stopped outside the hotel at three in the afternoon.[12] Then we tacked about from hotel to hotel, and every time we had to make an about-turn we had to drive on to a cross-roads in order to have turning space. First I was given a barrel as fellow passenger with a request from the driver to take good care of it since the coach heaved about rather unpleasantly. The lead horse threw himself from one side to the other and the many barrels and other baggage made me fear that the slender axles would soon break. Eventually we found another passenger and off we went to the neighbouring town of Lennoxville. On our way I observed labourers digging for copper and gold. A stamp mill was already in operation in Lennoxville. The horses were a good deal livelier than stage horses in Norway and Sweden, but I did not like the head horse they called Nigger. To avoid contact with the shaft that protruded between the two other horses he made all manner of free-style leaps.

Suddenly the strap that held Nigger's whippletree to the shaft snapped, the whippletree hit him on his hamstrings, and off we went in full gallop. The driver knew his mettle, however, and the horses were finally brought to a halt. We were lucky that the coach did not turn over. As soon as we arrived at the railway station in Lennoxville, however, a train came right towards us. The driver had just jumped down and when I saw Nigger lift his ears I was fast in following suit. No sooner had I reached *terra firma* than the horses were off at full career. The driver managed to hold on to the harness of one of the shaft horses while the other passenger held on with hands and feet looking out from the coach with a panicked expression. All disappeared and a full quarter of an hour passed by before the equipage returned, on four, two, and zero legs with the exception of two barrels, which had gone overboard, and the passenger, who had gone off on foot as soon as the horses stopped and who was not seen again. In less than a Norwegian mile I had thus been given a practical lesson in American transportation and from then on I would more frequently have my legs out in the open air so that I could jump off more easily before the horses ran off at full speed. Wherever I have travelled in America it has been my experience that there is little or no consideration for the passengers' comfort or safety in stage-coaches, and a fitting device for the stage companies to paint on their coaches would be "Not for pleasure alone."

After awhile two ladies and a screaming child took their places in the coach and we were back on the road, which was said to be in excellent condition, since it had been given its annual surface maintenance in the form of fill from the ditches just a few days earlier. For thirty miles we passed between cultivated fields of barley, oats, potatoes, and buckwheat. There seemed to be no ditches in the fields. The subsoil was sand and the land was not fit for wheat, regardless of the official reports on reliably good wheat harvests in the Eastern Townships. The buildings on the older farms were all of similar style, painted white and pleasant to look at and designed for a life in comfort. They looked much like the suburban dwellings in Homansbyen in Christiania. We passed by several large maple forests that are maintained as valuable resources since they provide sugar for domestic use as well as for sale on the market. The entire district had a pleasant appearance. At nightfall the fireflies swarmed in thousands like small Roman candles and hovered so densely around the horses' heads that their manes seemed to be on fire. These fireflies, which are mainly to be found on damp land and near forest, do not have the pale light of the glow-worm but radiate yellowish-golden beams when they fly. My faith in the superiority of Norwegian horses was never the same after this journey. Mile after mile the Canadian horses pulled the heavy stage-coach without stop. The thirty-mile-long and difficult road to the village of Robinson in Bury was traversed in five hours. Such a feat would have broken even the best Norwegian horses.

A HISTORY OF THE NORWEGIANS IN BURY

European emigrants seldom have more money than they need to get to their final destination. Therefore they cannot travel around in America, compare the respective qualities of various areas, and then freely choose the sites of their future homes. They will of necessity have to go by the reports and advice of others. In this manner the first group of Norwegian emigrants to Canada, led by an emigration agent, came to the border county of Compton just north of the state of Maine and settled on Company land in the town of Bury in 1856.[13] The land was, and to a great extent still is, forested. Depending on the quality of the land and the conditions of payment, they paid from $2.50 to $5.00 per acre. They cleared some land and built homes on it, but then after one or two years they left their clearings. Other Norwegians arrived, however, and moved into the abandoned houses. At one time twenty-three Norwegian families were settled here, but they continued to come and leave again until there were only six Norwegian families left in 1863. Some had been encouraged by the agent Closter[14] to go to Gaspé; others were smitten by the western fever, as it was called here, and went on to the north-western states.

The Norwegians were criticized for their lack of stability and their unwillingness to clear and cultivate their own farms. Instead of working on their own land at the most propitious time, they preferred to work for others, roaming far and wide for the cash that their wiser neighbours willingly paid them. When they had a few dollars they stayed at home, but instead of then working on their own land they simply relaxed. At midday one could find Norwegians smoking a pipe in bed, and they did not go out in search of work again until they had neither flour in the bin nor credit in the till. As an example of their laziness it was said that one of the families did not even bother to cut up the wood they had piled up outside their cabin for the winter. Instead they cut a hole through the bottom log of one of the walls of their cabin and dragged the log of firewood in through the hole so that one end could burn in the fireplace while the other was still out in the open. As the log was consumed by fire it was gradually pulled through the hole in the wall and could thus serve as firewood without having been exposed to saw or axe.

Young girls without stockings or shoes, but with garish silk parasols above their flower-decked straw hats, could be met on the roads. In the course of a couple of years, however, the Norwegians had saved enough money to pay for tickets for their families westward to Minnesota, while their land, with improvements, fences, and buildings, reverted to the Company. Even if they had not made much of a down payment, they nevertheless lost the value of whatever labour they had performed. Several families sold their chattel on credit and entrusted Saxlund with collection. Neither he nor any of the other Norwegians left in Bury have since heard from those who departed, and it is feared that they were among those who were killed during the Indian uprising in Minnesota in 1862.

I will list here some of the deserted farms that then were for sale at the original price, since my experience of Canada has led me to regard them as advantageous to the newcomer. One lot in the Eastern Townships is a hundred and forty-six acres.

Lot No. 22, Row 7, with a fairly good log cabin, ten acres of cleared land, an abundance of timber, a good maple forest, and water privileges on both sides of the river.

The north-eastern half of Lot No. 20 in the same row, abandoned by Zimmermann,[15] with a small house in good condition worth $50, three cultivated acres, a maple forest, and timber.

Lot No. 4, Row B, abandoned by the owner (Samson), with a poor cabin, twenty cultivated acres, a grove of maples, situated at a crossroads. Second-class soil.

Lot No. 26, Row 7, abandoned by Hardman. No buildings, five cultivated acres, a fairly good forest of maple. Second-class soil.

Lot No. 28, Row 8, abandoned by Locket. No buildings, eight cultivated acres, a good maple forest. First-class soil.

A lot abandoned by Peder Olsen, with a small cabin, two cultivated acres, but insufficient maple for production, and water privileges on both sides of the river. Second-class soil. The property is best suited for industrial use.

During my stay I was visited by a Terje Olsen from Risør,[16] who wanted my advice on selection of land. He was sent out to find land for three emigrant families. I had to tell him that I had not yet travelled sufficiently to give advice to emigrants. However, he had made up his mind to settle on forest land, and bought three lots with standing buildings abandoned by other Norwegians at $4.00 an acre. Each of these lots had a farmhouse as well as fields that would yield hay for three or four cows. The Company asked no instalments on the price for the first three years, but interest ran from the day of sale. Mr Buchanan, the government agent, paid $20 for the tickets from

Quebec to Bury for all three families. Thus they were able to save what money they had for cattle and hay. They came to ready-built houses, some cultivated land, and fields ready for cutting at no extra cost and could begin harvesting immediately. At the time these conditions seemed very favourable to me. Both a mill and a sawmill were close at hand. All of Canada is forest land and neither there nor in the United States have I seen any settlement with more promising prospects.

Contrary to this assessment is the fact that most of the Norwegians and even the emigration agent Haugan abandoned their land, having found them of little value and not to their liking. This departure is naturally of interest to the reader insofar as it leads me to investigate whether or not this part of Canada is suitable for settlement and cultivation. Research in this matter requires knowledge of North America's forests because the different kinds of trees are indicators of the character and quality of the soil. The forests may be divided into two main categories:

Softwood, such as pine, balsam, hemlock, spruce, and white cedar; that is, all kinds of evergreens or conifers

Hardwood, such as maple, elm, birch, beech, oak, ash, hickory, basswood, and butternut

The practical farmer in Canada has divided forest soil into four different categories depending on the growth of these trees on the land:

First-class soil is indicated by the dominance of maple, elm, birch, and beech.
Second-class soil has beech, birch, spruce, and hemlock.
Third-class soil has pine, spruce, hemlock, and cedar.
Fourth-class soil is bog and marshland with pine, spruce, and other conifers.
Tamaracks are only found on poor soil, but occur but seldom in the Eastern Townships.

First- and second-class soils are said to yield good harvests immediately after being cultivated, while third-class soil yields poor-to-middling harvests the first few years. The harvest improves, however, after all the stumps have been removed. In forest with a variety of trees, the soil is naturally best where hardwood is dominant.

The settler's choice of soil is decisive for his future welfare. Even though there was an abundance of both first- and second-class soil available in Bury (where the Land Company had four thousand acres for sale), the Scandinavians had generally selected second- and, above all, third-class soil. Thus they could not count on good harvests for the first years. In the dense forests there is hardly a blade of grass for grazing cattle, so during the first years the settler will not even have a supply of milk and meat from his clearing. The settler on forest land is faced with these serious disadvantages whether he goes to Canada or to the United States. Cattle may of course be able to survive for a winter on dry leaves and twigs that have been collected during the summer, but such fodder can only be a temporary solution in a crisis situation and can never be considered one of the advantages that America has compared to the Scandinavian countries.[17] The settler in a forest clearing without ready money for the first two years will consequently face a tough battle for survival. Certainly it is frequently said that the settler may burn potash and pay for his land with the returns from this industry, but this can only be done on hardwood-forest land (the ash of conifers will not do for potash). Even where the resources for such an industry are plentiful, however, it is so different from the work he is used to in the old country that he cannot count on the income he has been led to expect.

The emigration agent must be aware of these difficulties, and if he leads a poor emigrant family into the woods encouraging them to swing the pioneer's axe in virgin forest, this may mean either that he is inexperienced and without the necessary qualifications to serve helpless emigrants or that he has taken bribes from wealthy landowners to help them get buyers for their land. For my part, I would strongly advise against settling in virgin forest in any part of North America.

The case was different, however, for the Norwegians who had abandoned their farms in Bury. They had survived the first harsh pioneer years, had built their homes and cultivated some land. They left all of this for a new beginning somewhere else, while the Norwegians and Swedes who took over the abandoned properties were happy to be able to start off with homes they could move into and fields ready for cutting. I believe that the Norwegians who abandoned their farms in Bury did this partly because they were not professional farmers and partly because, tempted by the myth of quick success in the United States, they, like so many other thousands, had been led to release the bird in hand for the ten flying around above their heads. If future emigrants arriving in Quebec should receive information about vacant farms with buildings in the Eastern Townships, I would advise them to settle there if they do not have the funds to travel to the prairies of the Far West.[18] It is also of great advantage to the farmer that farm products are far higher priced in eastern Canada than twelve hundred miles farther west, where the farmer must pay the cost of transportation to the coast.

ADVENTURES IN THE VIRGIN FOREST

In spite of the dark sides of pioneer life in the primeval forest, every year thousands of emigrants prefer it to the sparsely forested prairies or the so-called "clearings" between scattered oaks. In Canada forest land can be bought for from 25 cents to $1.00 an acre. The emigrant without money should not buy land but first save sufficient funds to allow him to work on his own land rather than that of his neighbours. A labourer's hire in Lower Canada is from $10 to $12 a month besides free bed and board. So a bachelor should be able to set aside $60 in six months and for this he could buy a hundred acres of government land (good hardwood land) at a price of 60 cents an acre. Raising a log cabin will cost him $20. The trees he cuts down the first summer should be burnt the following spring before sowing. Thus he will be able to supplement his own fare and feed his cow a year after he has begun working. The first harvest will often fail, and this may be because of the quality of the soil, but I have observed that in nine out of ten cases the settler himself must bear the blame. Either he has tried to burn his clearing before the trees he has cut down are sufficiently dry or he has set fire to them so late in the spring that it is too late for sowing, or, and this is the worst, he has neglected to sow in the land he has cleared and as a consequence there is such a dense growth of weeds that the land reverts to an uncultivated state and will require intense work before grass or grain can be harvested. I saw a Norwegian clearing of twenty acres that lay waste and abandoned because the work on it had not been done at the right time. Emigrants who have not been involved in agriculture in the old country should bear in mind that the move to America is not alone sufficient to make them good farmers. They should refrain from cultivating their own land until they have learned the methods from others.

The government demands at least one-fifth of the price in cash, but there are two ways of getting land without an immediate down payment. You can find yourself a section of land, build on it, and put off reporting it to the governmental agent until you have the means to pay for it. This is called squatting. But this procedure may turn out to be a costly affair for the squatter because a speculator may find out what he has done and then run off to the government agent and buy the land. The agent would not have sold the land to a speculator had he known that there was a squatter but would first have offered it to him at the original price. The speculator, however, will now demand many times that sum or force the squatter off the land he has cleared and built on.

You may also go direct to the agent and let him know what land you have decided to buy. Payment within six months will count as cash payment. The first instalment for a hundred acres is $15, so it is relatively easy for a poor emigrant to acquire land. In this connection I would warn against paying for people's passage across the Atlantic to be repaid in labour after their arrival. For a family of four the tickets, including meals, on a sailing ship would amount to from $80 to $100. Such contracts are, generally speaking, not recognized by the courts. Since the head of the family that has received this assistance will have so little difficulty in acquiring his own land, he will not have the patience to put in from eighty to a hundred days of labour on another's farm, especially considering the fact that his family also depends on his labour.

The townships of Bury, Newport, Lingwick, and a part of Mégantic have excellent hardwood land with a soil free of rocks. In Dudswell the land is more hilly than in Bury.

On 7 July Pennoyer, Tambs, his son, and I had agreed to take a several days' tour of the Company's forests. With a piece of rope Pennoyer turned my woollen blanket into an Indian knapsack capable of holding our belongings, mainly food and cooking utensils. We started off following the arrow-straight roads of the settlement for the first few miles. The topsoil was mostly mould and, below, there was either porous clay or sand, except for a few areas with limestone in between. The Scots were the best farmers. Fields of timothy were seen everywhere. On a seventy-five-acre clearing I saw timothy that was fourteen years old, but it had now become so sparse that it was not worth cutting and merely served as pasture.

After some miles we came to the home of a farmer named James Ward, to whom I am indebted for some of the following information. He was an educated man and had lived on his land for twenty-seven years, and therefore his experience should be of some value. He had cleared seventy of his hundred and forty-six acres, and these now fed his family. Haying had just begun, but his timothy was not yet at full growth. He had fifteen head of cattle and spread the manure on four acres every year, and this is about the same distribution of fertilizer common on Norwegian farms in Oppland.[19] He was, like all others, ignorant of the use of compost, but was ready to accept its value. Eighty years ago a storm had blown down much of the original forest over a large area, and now a forest of young maples had grown up in its stead. Since the trunks were only from four to nine inches thick at the root, Ward insisted that the land was very easy to clear and that the stumps would rot in six to seven years' time, thus making the land ready for the plough. Ward took us through large areas of gently sloping hardwood land with first-class soil, and he claimed that a property of one hundred acres, most of it cultivated and the rest cleared for forest, could not be had for less than $3,000, or $30 an acre. Of this sum, however, $10 an acre would be for buildings and fences. In addition, each lot should include fifty acres of forest, including about four hundred sugar maples with an annual yield of two to two and a half pounds of sugar from each tree. He had not found that tapping caused damage to the trees; he had been tapping for at least ten years.

The accounts for his farm, worth $3,000, with one hundred acres cultivated land and forty-six acres of forest and sugar maple, was as follows:

EXPENSES

Annual interest on $3000.00	$180.00
Taxes	$ 20.00
Hired labour: Two adult labourers at $125 each	$250.00
Two maids at $50 each	$100.00
One boy	$ 60.00
Farm equipment: Interest on estimated value at $125	$ 15.00
Annual depreciation and repairs	$ 50.00
Household expenses: Food and drink for the help mentioned above and for a family of five based on average market prices over the last three years, for ten persons at $50 per person	$500.00
Horses: 500 bushels of oats, two tons of hay, and pasture at $5 per horse, for two horses	$ 75.00
Sugar shed and equipment for the sugar harvest: interest on $120	$ 7.00
Depreciation	$ 7.00
Sum	$1,306.00

INCOME

Sugar from 400 trees at 2½ pounds per tree = 1,000 pounds at $7 per 100 pounds	$ 70.00
Fodder: hay from 30 acres = 45 tons, which gives a return of $6 per ton when used through the winter for cattle and sheep	$270.00
straw and greens of root crops, which gives a return of $3 per acre as fodder	$ 90.00

Seed: 27 acres of a variety of grains, which, on the basis of a
   good oats harvest, gives 40 bushels per acre at 1 shilling
   & 9 pence per bushel = $14 per acre, amounting to $378.00
Potatoes: 1¹/₂ acres, 200 bushels per acre at 25 cents a bushel $ 75.00
Turnips: 1¹/₂ acres, 500 bushels per acre, which gives a return
   of $10 per bushel as fodder $ 75.00
Pasture: 40 acres of meadows and 46 acres of forest land in
   six months for 50 sheep, 10 cows, 10 heifers, equals
   the profits on the winter fodder $360.00
(The total value of fodder for the full year, $720.00, for the
   farm's livestock can be broken down as follows:

From 2 horses, approx.	$ 20.00
wool and lambs of 50 sheep	$200.00
butter from 10 cows	$200.00
10 heifers at $20 each	$200.00
milk	$100.00
Sum	$720.00

Pork: annual product of garbage $ 50.00
Forest: The value of the forest would be impaired if used for
   anything but fences and firewood. Moreover, lumber is
   hardly marketable $000.00
Sum $1,368.00

The net profit of a farm of one hundred acres cultivated land and forty-six acres forest amounts to $62 if all help is hired and the farmer is merely a superviser. I believe that these accounts come fairly close to the truth, even though I am aware that some will object to the small net profit I have arrived at.

It should be brought to mind, however, that the main income of the farmer class of all countries is derived from the labour of the farmer and his family. Consequently, when the farmer, his wife, and his children do the work instead of hiring help, it should be possible to save $235 in wages and $150 in food. If this is added to the net profit of the farm, the total will be $447. So gentleman farming is as unprofitable in Canada as in Norway,[20] but the farmer who works his own farm can own his own land in a shorter time and for less money than in the latter country. Ward estimated that the work that he and his family did on the farm was worth about $300 a year.

It is scarcely profitable to concentrate on sheep alone on forest land. It should be possible to collect enough hay in the clearings for the winter, but there is no good summer pasture in the forest. Along the rivers there may be meadowlike land where thousands of cattle may be fed, but these pastures are too damp for sheep, which require dry pastures if illness is to be avoided. So in Canada sheep are kept mostly in connection with general farming. Large-scale speculation on sheep alone is a feature of the western prairies, where shepherds can move around freely with their tents and light camp gear through the whole summer on rich pastureland and return to the farm in the fall and there feed their flock through the winter. In this part of Canada a fully grown sheep costs $4.00, a lamb in the fall $2.25, and wool can be sold at 30 cents a pound. One ton of hay will feed three sheep through the winter.

While Company land cannot be bought for less than $3.00 an acre, government land of the same quality may be had for 60 cents an acre. Mr Farwell, the government agent, has much land for sale in the Eastern Townships. If price is the only consideration, government land is obviously to be preferred, but if one can acquire both a house and cleared land on Company land and in addition have a short way to a mill, sawmill, and church, these advantages are so important that it would be worthwhile to pay a higher initial price for the land.

For emigrants who prefer government land the following information may be helpful: The price for one hundred acres of Company land is at least $300. Of this sum no down payment is required on purchase, but there is an annual interest of $18. After having paid $12 a year for five years the buyer of government land will have paid for his land in full, while the settler who has bought Company land will have paid $90 in interest and still not have come any closer to owning his land.

There are some Canadian members of Parliament who are genuinely concerned about the problems of settlers on government land. When at a later date I went to the village of Cookshire in the town of Eaton to meet the member of Parliament, Mr Pope,[21] he showed me a plan to benefit the emigrant that he would try to get support for. His idea was that money raised by a financing company through subscription could be used to advance money to the emigrant who wanted to settle on government land. This company would have experienced consultants who could show the settler how to put his forest to profitable use by burning salt and potash. The company would enter into a contract with the settler: "For each cultivated acre he shall be awarded two-thirds of the costs as a loan. In repayment the settler shall let the company have part of his products." In this manner the company would have its money returned and could put it to use again to further the cultivation of government land.

But let me return to our tour of the forests.

We were blessed with the most beautiful weather that lasted far into the afternoon. The heat, however, was oppressive and the mosquitoes were so hungry for our blood, even at mid-day, that we had to wave green branches about our ears much in the way the horse uses his tail. We progressed through the gigantic forest, climbing over four-foot-thick windfalls and crossing gently running brooks. Every half-hour we had to take a spell from our exertions, but we would have had no rest had we not started a fire to keep the mosquitoes away. In spite of the powerful sun we had to lean so close to the fire that the mosquitoes found the approach too risky. When we resumed our journey our guide took a smoky brand from the fire and led the way. The others followed "Indian file" to benefit from the smoke. We all longed for evening when at least we would not have the sun beating down on us, but quite unexpectedly we were suddenly cooled down in a manner I will long remember. The sky, which the dense forest had kept from our view, suddenly darkened as if by magic. Lightning followed lightning and the rain poured down in torrents. We gathered together in a group and held up my woollen blanket as a tent above our heads to protect us from the water. Thus we stood for an hour and each time one of us ventured out he was met by lightning and spurts of water. The forest resounded with sighs and clashes. Many trees were struck by lightning; others were felled by the powerful wind. We had planned to camp that night in the forest, but this was out of the question. No campfire could be made to burn, and a severe cold would have been a consequence of lying down on the wet ground and being soaked from below as well as from above. Our guide knew of a cabin four miles farther on and we decided to try to reach it before it became pitch-dark.

If my reader had been with us in our flight from the raging elements I think that in the future he would have refrained from taking walks through the forest. The storm had made lakes of large stretches of one-time land, and we often had to wade up to our knees in water. None escaped an additional total immersion when the foot slipped or was taken unawares by sudden depressions. Towards the end of our wandering we came to a fence that had been torn down by the storm. On the other side, in a hollow, was a cabin that was to give us protection, but between us was a brook that now had grown to a river that had swept away the bridge. We had no choice but to enter the river and swim across. The owner of the cabin, Mr. McAdam, and his wife (McEva?) received us kindly under their roof, which to us seemed a paradise since we were exhausted, hungry, and sleepy and had lost our food in the flood and now had expectations of satisfying our bodily needs.

Even though such sudden changes in the weather do not happen daily here in America, as claimed by another traveller, they are nevertheless so common that the farmer must be prepared to risk them every year.

The next day we went on to Lake Moffat, where an English captain spent his annual income in fishing, cultivating the soil, and building a manor house.[22] The flat land surrounding most of the lake was mostly swamp, but the shore was set with stones in some places. The same is true of other lakes in the Eastern Townships. The approach to the lake was difficult and we did not arrive until half an hour before dark. Since the transition from light to dark is so sudden, we all had to concentrate on getting ready for the night. Bark was flaked off large conifers and served as a roof. The water in the lake was so lukewarm that it was unfit for drinking, so we had to dig for water in the forest, and even if this water was muddy and black, we preferred it because it was cold. We also had to keep a fire burning to keep away the night fog as well as the mosquitoes. We cut logs that we pulled up to our fire, and erected a wall that directed the smoke under our bark roof. While it certainly was not very comfortable to breathe in this acrid smoke all night, it was nevertheless preferable to being eaten by the swarms of mosquitoes that had discovered the smell of human blood. Owls, swans, and the loud-spoken bullfrogs cried all night, so I for one was relieved when dawn finally vanquished all this cacophony.

In order to cross the lake we now cut logs for a small raft and covered it with a deck made of the bark from our roof. My blanket served as a sail, a pole as a mast, and another pole as a rudder; but since the raft could only take two of us at a time, Cornelius Tambs and I set out alone to manœuvre it across to the Englishman's property, where we hoped to borrow a boat that could take the rest of our company across the lake. The voyage, however, could well have turned out to be our last. The ropes that bound our four logs loosened and the waves swept off the bark so that we had to sit down and use arms and legs to keep the raft from falling apart. The makeshift mast fell down several times and finally we decided to give up sailing, immerse the lower part of our bodies in the water, and drift according to wind and current. But our fear that the raft would break apart completely or that we would have to spend the whole night out on the lake led us to renew our exertions. The mast was raised again and Cornelius held it with both hands while I worked hard with the other pole to keep us close to the wind. Finally we succeeded in reaching the other shore, where the Englishman and his guests had assembled to get a closer look at the characters they had observed through their spyglass, half in half out of the water, manœuvring towards their beach. He kept the raft as a curiosity and treated us to food and drink. He even offered Cornelius, whose skills he had so admired, $300 and free board if he would stay with him, go fishing with him, and do odd jobs around the house.

I can hear my reader objecting: What is this water story doing in a book that is supposed to give information on Canada? My answer must be that if I had not escaped from this water adventure with my life I would not have had the pleasure of again putting pen to paper in this world. Moreover, future Norwegian tourists will learn that they must be prepared for anything if they venture into the forest on their journey. Finally, the reader must bear with an author who cannot forget the thorns he stepped on in his endeavours to pick roses for his readers.

The next day we met a group of settlers who had set out to spend a few weeks clearing their lots in the forest. The custom here is to cut down as much timber as possible in the summer while the leaves are green, since the leaves will make it easier to burn the trees when they are dry. It takes about six weeks for the trees to become sufficiently dry for burning, and the fires are set all over Canada on 1 September. In most clearings oats are sown in the ashes the following spring, since this is in all circumstances the safest and most bountiful species of grain.

Before I leave the Eastern Townships I must give an account of the vegetation as I observed it on 1 July. The meadows were mainly of timothy and clover. The timothy ears varied from two to four inches but they had not yet flowered out in the country. (Close to the towns, of course, the vegetation was further advanced.) This grass seems to thrive particularly well here. Even on neglected stump clearings the timothy was dense between the raspberry canes. Since the meadows have never been fertilized with manure but have merely been sown in the ashes, an acre does not yield more hay here than in Norway, but the dark green of the grass and the length of the ears indicated that the hay was generally of a better quality than that from the meadows of Norway.[23] Barley and oats had grown nice ears; corn had not yet grown to full length in the country, while around Lennoxville it was both at full length and in full flower. That corn thrives and beech trees can often grow to giant size are reliable evidence that the climate of this part of Canada is by far more beneficent than that of southern Norway. Wild fruit trees were not often to be seen in the forest; in fact I can only remember seeing apple trees and red currants, and never grape vines.

People seemed healthy and I was told that the so-called "*ague and fever*" was unknown in these parts, while there were reports on how this disease was rampant among the Scandinavians in the United States. There was good water everywhere. Of the neighbouring republic, however, it was said that the water, in particular on the prairies and on most farms in the West, was so poor and so filled with insects that it could not be enjoyed except when holding your nose and closing your eyes. I was later to discover from my own experience that both the fever and the rotten water to a great extent were myths and that such horror tales are told in Canada to encourage the emigrant to stop and not continue on his way to the West. The schoolmaster in Bury, Mr Cooly, informed me that sudden death had often struck among the Scandinavians immediately after their arrival. The reason was assumed to be the poor conditions and the diet during the Atlantic crossing, followed by an excessive drinking of water and strenuous work in the hot climate of the Eastern Townships. On our return I discovered a makeshift smelting works in Lennoxville. The copper ore held 4 per cent copper. While working hard in the heat the workers not only drank water but threw handfuls of uncooked oatmeal into the bucket and stirred it each time they drank. It was claimed that this mixture made the large amount of water they drank harmless. I give this as advice to farmers who may want to follow this example during the harvest when the excessive drinking of cold water has made labourers sick.

I was well received in the home of the Norwegian Mr Tambs. He went with me on several tours and gave me much information. In his home I learned how comfortable life can be made, even in a far-away place, when the members of the family have the spiritual gifts that give peace and happiness.

FROM RICHMOND TO QUEBEC:
GOVERNMENT AGENTS

For almost a hundred miles, from Richmond to Quebec, the road passed through a landscape of broad fields, often with spruce and cedar. The soil was sandy and neither grass nor grains had yet formed spikes. The population was mainly French. The cattle were smaller and not as well fed as in the Eastern Townships, where the milk cows looked as good as the best cows in Norway. English breeds of sheep were dominant; there were no merinos even though the grass and the climate would seem suitable for them. The last stretch of the road, from Bécancour to Quebec, passed through lowlands that were quite flat and without any hills, not unlike the unflooded parts of the marshes at the northern end of Lake Øyeren in Norway.[24] Since the emigrant is in search of soil that is better than that of the land he left behind, I cannot recommend settlement in this area.

Finally, on 15 July, I was once more in Quebec, where I could take a much-needed rest for a few days, see to my clothes, which had received rather rough treatment in the wilderness, and prepare for a new journey on both sides of the St Lawrence towards the sea.

In Quebec many of the aggressive emigration agents had set up their quarters for the summer.[25] Their business consists partly of persuading the emigrants to settle in specific areas and partly of selling them tickets for the railroads and steamship companies they represent. Much has been said and written about the alleged harm these agents have done to emigrants, who are totally ignorant of conditions in their new country. Some of these complaints are reasonable, but to a great extent they are either without basis in fact or unmerited, because the main fault lies with the emigrants themselves. The English government has appointed a main agent whose duty it is to look after the needs of those who cross the Atlantic from Great Britain.[26] His clerks boarded every ship and inquired whether there were any there who wished to settle in Canada. Those who responded were given free transportation to the place of their choice and, if they were destitute, $5.00 each to help them on their way.

Among the agent's duties was finding good homes for young women who were on their own, and he was most conscientious in taking care of this.[27] Citizens of Quebec appeared daily to acquire servants, but they were refused entrance even to the agency building where the single women could have free board and lodgings until suitable employment had been found for them in Canada.[28] "In Quebec," Mr Buchanan would admonish these women, "many will want to keep you only during the busy summer months and then you will be left on your own when winter comes." Scandinavian women should also mark his words.

The English agent, however, did not take care of only his countrymen; whenever possible he also tried to be of assistance to needy Scandinavians. But the number of destitute Norwegian and Swedish emigrants has been so large in recent years that the English agency has had to announce that they could no longer count on any help if they did not plan to settle in Canada. Our own consul can do nothing for them since no funds have been allotted for such work. The Scandinavians have no representatives in any of the major American ports who can address themselves to their problems.

Other agents in the service of the major land or mining companies also engage both individuals and entire families to go west under their wings. Since so many of the emigrants are too poor to pay for their own journey and since there is no profitable employment to be had in the city of Quebec, they will often choose this alternative as a way of acquiring free passage westward. I believe that the ensuing complaints about bad treatment from the company in whose service they have enlisted may be ascribed to the fact that the emigrants themselves have not entered their contract with the company in good faith. They long for their family and friends in other parts of America and eagerly grasp any opportunity to have their contract annulled. But they soon discover that there is no escape from the difficulties of a settler on new land, regardless of whether they are working for themselves or for others.

If emigrants with sufficient means are enticed to enter contracts for the purchase of land held by companies or speculators simply because they are ignorant of cheaper or better alternatives, this is of course deplorable, but from this date they themselves must take the blame for their actions. For now it is no longer difficult for anyone who can read in his own language to acquire the necessary information. I would nevertheless discourage the emigrant from placing trust in the pamphlets or leaflets that promote the excellence of particular states or districts, certainly not because I would like to advertise this little book, but because it is a well-known fact that the authors of most of these pamphlets have been paid for their labours.

CHAPTER 4

From Quebec Eastward
to the Sea

—— ∴ ——

While my first journey from Quebec had been towards the south-west,[1] I now travelled towards the north-east; that is, in the opposite direction, but still on the south side of the St Lawrence River. The Eastern Townships are situated between forty-five and forty-six degrees north latitudes. The area I was now going to explore is between forty-seven and forty-nine degrees north latitudes; that is, about the same latitude as Lake Superior.

It is not so much its northerly position as its cold ocean winds and mountainous character that make this region less attractive for farming. Some miles from the river there are gently sloping plains as far as the eye can see. Agriculture was nevertheless in its infancy. There were hardly any ditches in the fields. The soil was excellent clay in some areas, sand or bog in others. Large hills were more or less strewn with rocks and boulders. Timothy thrived and was in flower on 17 July. Other main crops were oats, barley, wheat, buckwheat, and potatoes. I did not discover any cornfields. The fields were sparse and weedy and were often overgrown with wild buckwheat. To me the land seemed best suited for cattle, but I did not see much meadowland. The land that had been cultivated reminded me of the rocky plains of Västergotland in Sweden and was surrounded by hills on the horizon. Even though poor agricultural methods may be to blame for the poor appearance of the land, the absence of corn nevertheless suggested that there was not enough productive warmth for such crops. Most industry in the small towns by the river was based on either the sea or the forest. Most of the forest was evergreen, and where there was a mixture of evergreens and hardwood the soil was always claimed to be excellent. By Norwegian standards it was truly excellent; but measured according to the soil classification for forest land presented earlier in these pages, even the best areas must be placed in the third and fourth classes.

Almost four hundred miles northeast of Quebec, where the land meets the sea, there was an attempt some years ago to establish a Norwegian settlement in the Gaspé region.[2] Here, as on so many stretches of the coast, there are salt-water fisheries on a large scale. The prevailing belief was that the Norwegians, who were used to the sea and a harsh climate, would be better equipped than any other nation to profit from a settlement in such an area. The project, how-ever, was a total failure. The Norwegians had neither the capital nor the experience for American-style fisheries, and the crops on their small clearings were ruined by early-autumn frost. As soon as they were able to obtain the necessary money for the journey, they went on to the West, cursing Canada from the bottom of their hearts. The Canadian government has had reason to regret this colonization attempt, which has cast such an undeserved shadow over all of Canada. Most emigrants from Norway are totally ignorant of geography, so when they hear mention of Canada, they think the whole country is like Gaspé. If our countrymen were cheated when they were lured to Gaspé, many took their revenge when they left. There was, for instance, a group of sixty men and women who boarded a coastal steamer to go to Quebec. The vessel had already sailed a good many miles when the ticket seller went his rounds on deck to collect money from the passengers. There they sat, the sixty Norwegians, all in a row, and each and every one refused to pay. The ticket seller could not get a single cent from them, and he had to report to the captain that they all, as the ballad goes, had a full heart but an empty wallet. The captain was so impressed by the audacity of the Norwegians that he roared with laughter and took them all the four hundred miles to Quebec without charge, *gratis and for nothing*.[3]

The entire region I travelled through was settled exclusively by the French. All over Canada, not only do the French differ from the English in religion and in language, but they also strive to maintain and even to increase their own national group. In this they are assisted by an active clergy, and the French population increases spectacularly each year. It is a hardier race than any other in Canada and it expands rapidly in regions in which the English as well as the Scandinavians decline. Consequently, the regions east of Quebec will become exclusively French and the Scandinavians would be ill advised to settle among a race so radically different from their own.

It would have been interesting for a forest speculator with capital to travel through the country eastward to Gaspé, since the trade in lumber, both domestic and with England, is lively, but for me it would have been wasted time and energy to go farther east since in no circum-stances would I be able to recommend this outlying region of Canada to my countrymen. So after having penetrated part of the Rimouski

Territory, about a hundred and seventy miles from Quebec, I returned to Rivière-du-Loup to cross the St Lawrence River and enter the country north of the river on the so-called "Labrador" side.

Tired and fed up with being rattled about in Canadian gigs for the last few days, I got off at the bathing resort of Cacouna, the favourite summer spot for the ladies of Quebec, and walked the last five miles to the steamship wharf.[4] Along the road Indians had set up some birch-bark tents, and since I have always felt sympathy for these unyielding original inhabitants of America, I made use of this opportunity to engage them in conversation.[5] The tents housed three males, one of whom was a chief more than a hundred years old, and twenty-three squaws, or widows, as they referred to themselves. In what manner all these women in their best age had entered respectable widowhood I could not discover. In all probability these daughters of nature went in and out of matrimony every month. They were diligent at their basketwork, for which there apparently was a good market.[6] The old chief was bad tempered and refused to reveal his name because he believed that I had evil intentions. A policeman had recently tricked him into giving him his name and then fined him for catching salmon out of season: "When the white man's law allows us to fish they keep all salmon and trout away from our rivers by blocking them with their nets. Thus the Indian is prevented from catching fish for his dinner. When they take away their nets and the fish again can enter our rivers, the white man says that it is illegal for us to catch them. In this manner we are exposed to starvation and we therefore have to move around and set up our tents wherever money can be made from the insignificant skills of our women. In earlier times we owned much land, but now the Maliseet tribe is poor and becomes weaker every year."[7]

I spent the night in the attic of a French fisherman's cabin along with the wardrobe of three girls. These beauties themselves slept in another building, but I wish they had taken all their belongings with them so that I could have had a more peaceful night. I begged the fleas to forget I was there, wrapped myself up in my old grey blanket, and slept fitfully until my host woke me at dawn with the news that the *Magnet* was in sight. That quickly pulled me out of bed and down to breakfast. Among the courses there was a kind of seaweed that later that day I saw people chewing as a kind of delicacy. To me it tasted like salty, fibrous lettuce and as I am not particularly fond of eating grass, I missed the exquisite pleasure of this treat.[8]

CHAPTER 5

Up the Saguenay River
to Lake St Jean

At six in the morning the *Magnet* blew its whistle for departure and set out across the almost twelve-mile-wide St Lawrence for the town of Tadoussac at the mouth of the Saguenay River.[1] We crossed the river in heavy fog and ice-cold winds and were happy to come in the lee of hills on the north shore and get protection from the cold breath of the Hudson Bay and Greenland. Many of the passengers were tourists from western Canada who wanted to see the Saguenay and its surroundings. There is not much to admire for the person who has seen the proud mountains of Norway. The hills on either side of the river seemed to be about two hundred to three hundred feet high and even the coast of Labrador rises from only two hundred to four hundred feet above sea level. But the Saguenay was different from all other rivers I have seen in that the hills fell steeply down to the water, not leaving the slightest strip of land along the banks where a real fisherman's cabin could have been tufted or where the imagination could have created an idyllic spot.

While our boat lay in Tadoussac to load birchwood for fuel we took advantage of the opportunity to explore the town. The houses are squeezed in between large sandbanks and the naked cliffs in the background. The view of the river was the town's only attraction until it acquired new interest for me with a sign I discovered on one of the buildings that looked somewhat like a deserted meeting-house. In gilded letters I read: MR PRICE, ROYAL NORWEGIAN AND SWEDISH CONSUL FOR SAGUENAY.[2] This was the first time I had ever seen the name of Norway mentioned before that of Sweden in an official context. When I later broached this subject with Mr Price he explained that in the entire Quebec region as well as in his own large business he saw virtually only Norwegian ships; therefore he found it natural that the country that in Canada was regarded as a more important maritime

nation than Sweden should be mentioned first. Swedish gentlemen
had indeed rebuked him on occasion but he saw no reason to make
any change if the Norwegian government did not encourage him to
do so.

The passengers were not very lively considering that they were tourists. The gentlemen fussed around their own ladies and had the air
of sole proprietors, and the eternal shadows in the drapes of death,
the Catholic priests, were sufficient unto themselves. They spoke to
no one and no one to them. They can travel wherever they wish without charge, and make good use of this privilege. Because of the rapid
current we often had to cross from one bank to the other but the view
was nevertheless monotonous. It was as if nature had set out to create
something splendid but that a natural revolution had come along with
a drawknife and cut off all protruding rock formations. An exception
to this were the two cliffs called Eternity and Trinity[3] and the steamship always passes close to both of them to entertain the passengers
with the powerful and repeated echo of the steam whistle. We met
no other vessels on the mighty river except for canoes with dark
brown Indians that would occasionally glide past us.

An Episcopal clergyman from Toronto seemed very interested in
Scandinavian emigration to Canada. He assured me that the Episcopal
bishop for the region in question would provide the Norwegian clergy
with the necessary support from year to year, but insisted that these
ministers would have to confess the Episcopal faith. I tried to explain
to him that this would be impossible for the clergy as well as for their
congregation, but he could not accept that there could be any reason
for our clergy to stand by their Lutheran faith other than the loss of
the right to a calling in the old country.[4]

Later in the afternoon we turned into a several-mile-long fjord to
the left and lay to in a wide bay called Ha! Ha! Bay. The bay had been
given its strange name by its first discoverer, who had entered this
fjord believing he had found the main artery of the Saguenay, and then
laughed at his own mistake when he came into the bay. Lake St-Jean
was a long way off, so I did not hesitate to enter a gig along with a
Catholic priest and headed for Lake Kénogami.

Around the bay there was clay in the soil, but after a few miles' drive
we came to a sandy area that stretched as far as the eye could see.
Here the pine forest for miles around had been destroyed by fire. In
all forested areas the settler runs the risk of having his home burnt
down in the frequent forest fires that in their fierceness can be compared to prairie fires. For this reason the settler often first raises a
shanty[5] in which he lives until he has cleared so much of the forest
that a fire cannot reach his buildings. Along the numerous forks of

the river the soil was fertile. At this time the grass stood as tall as it had done in the Eastern Townships eight days earlier, but the potatoes were smaller. There were fine fields of barley, but no corn. Winter rye is an unknown variety, while the poorer spring rye is grown on most farms. Wheat was rare. Between the many rivers, which ran from fifty to eighty feet below, there was uninterrupted tableland. The French had settled here so long ago that the area had the appearance of old farmland, not of clearings. The population could not understand a single word of English and had no sympathy for the Anglo-Saxon tribe that had penetrated Canada.

Towards nightfall we climbed into a birch-bark canoe that was to take us the whole length of Lake Kénogami, which is connected to the great Lake St-Jean by a small river. This is the route the Hudson's Bay Company uses to carry freight to its outpost on Lake St-Jean. We were six people huddled together at the bottom of this nutshell with so little space that we could not move, and had we tried to change places, the canoe would surely have capsized. The French Canadians who paddled the canoe entertained us with dialogue ballads and the priest and I had plenty to talk about. Among other things I asked him if he was married, pretending ignorance of the rule of celibacy. With great seriousness he replied in the negative and explained at some length the old doctrine that matrimony would draw the clergy's thoughts to the material welfare of their own family rather than to the spiritual welfare of their flock. I described the life of a clergyman's family in Norway and explained that, contrary to our actual experience, where the government has provided the clergy with a decent salary, thoughts of material matters do not take up their time. The family life of the clergy served as an example for their congregation, and their children, who were always in the view of the congregation, were brought up in the spirit of Christian humility. Any educated man would want a clergyman's daughter as his life companion because he realized that the good family life of a clergyman brought blessings both to those nearest him and to those of his congregation who chose to follow his example. The poor Catholic, who had forsworn womankind, looked down and admitted that it could be possible that I was right.

The night was dark and when it also began to rain steadily we decided to seek shelter for the night in the first dwelling we came to, whether it belonged to a white or a red man. A light beckoned in the forest. We got out of the canoe and approached a birch-bark tent where five dogs tried to discourage us from going any farther. The tent housed an old French Canadian, his Indian wife, and two other Indians. The household was now increased not only by our party of six from the canoe but by the five dogs as well. The animals placed themselves next to the fire of coals at the centre of the tent and the humans circled around them, with the priest and me closest to the wall where we gasped for air at the cracks: The heat and the sickening smells increased minute by minute. The pleasant conversation was about fish, moose, and deer and went on for a few hours until the canoe paddlers declared that it was time for us to be on our way again and we continued towards Hébertville.

To begin with, the shores of the lake were virtually uninhabited but at the upper half it was again lined with French settlements. At the other end of the lake our paddlers carried the canoe on their backs to a river by which we sailed to Lake St-Jean. The forest consisted mainly of spruce and birch except where it had burnt down. Here the second growth was exclusively of aspen. In Norway, aspen is not a good indication of fertile soil and a mild climate, and surely this holds true here as well. However, this should not be construed to mean that the land surrounding Lake St-Jean – for instance the townships of Laterrière and Chicoutimi – suffers from a harsh climate because of its northerly location. The vegetation and the exceptional slimness and height of the trees compared to the trees in Norwegian forests were evidence of the fact that both soil and climate are the equal of, if not superior to, that of Norway's Oppland County, and it is an accepted fact that the climate around Lake St-Jean is far milder than that of the land around Quebec, even though the latter lies farther south. The mountain ranges in the north, north-east, and north-west that frame this landscape are an effective barrier to the cold winds that otherwise would have influenced the vegetation. The land to the west and south of the shores of Lake St-Jean has been taken. To the north and east the land has a sandy and infertile soil and is still a wilderness. I could not possibly go round the entire lake by canoe since it is twenty miles long and twenty-five miles across and the waves are larger than a canoe can manage. So my own observations were necessarily limited and for the most part I had to rely on what others could tell me about the quality of the land.

The return trip overland to the town of Chicoutimi, forty miles from Lake St-Jean, went through wilderness as well as settled areas. Our driver drove his gig like a madman, as if to demonstrate how much punishment his Quebec gig and horse could take. These gigs have two seats and can take four passengers. The driver sits up front, right behind the horse's tail. The wheels went over a succession of holes, roots, rocks, corduroy roads,[6] and windfalls. "*March, marche donc, sacré Providence*" ("Giddyap, giddyap, by God"), our driver called out to his horse every minute. Most of the land along the road was taken. For miles on end there were enormous birch forests, but a recent forest fire had cut off the thread of life at the root and now the tall and slender white trunks stood with their leafless crowns against the blue sky, giving the impression of a winter landscape on a green base. In between the birch forests there were stretches of aspen, pine, and spruce. Ten years earlier an exceptionally cold spring had killed all maples and fruit trees in the environs of Lake St-Jean as well as on both banks of the Saguenay River as far down as Chicoutimi. These low spring temperatures had affected all of Lower Canada and killed fruit trees as far south as the Eastern Townships. Maples were spared here, however.

The soil consisted partly of a fertile reddish sand and partly, in particular towards the end of our journey, of black mould. The yield of the soil can be compared to that of eastern Norway. While the fields of rye, because of the poor variety used, were so sparse, that the harvest would hardly be profitable, the peas and oats looked fine, even though there were weeds and grass among the peas. Barley had not yet awned, but the peas were in flower. Cattle (cows) were normal in size but there seemed to have been little improvement in the breed. Agriculture was based on soil exhaustion: Single crops were grown until the land could yield no more. Nowhere did the farmers save manure and use it as fertilizer on their fields. Even though pastures bordered on fields and buildings, the cattle were always free to roam. Fifty feet or so from the farm buildings there was usually a small clay baking oven about three feet long. It rested on a three-foot-high wooden stand and looked like a horizontal queen bee cell in a beehive.

Towards evening we rolled down steep hills to the mighty Saguenay River. As we came down from the tableland into the valley the landscape acquired a more mountainous character, with large deforested areas in the vicinity of the mill town Chicoutimi. I was received with unexpected hospitality by the Norwegian–Swedish consul, Mr Price. I had been on the road continuously since my last departure from Quebec, and I was happy to accept his kind invitation to stay for a time in his home. The consul had a considerable lumber business with England. Twenty or so Norwegian ships were loaded every summer at his docks here and in Ha! Ha! Bay. Many a Norwegian seaman, after having seen only wilderness for hundreds of miles, with signs here and there of the first attempts at civilization, will have memories of the impression made by the harbour installations along the river and the white buildings of Chicoutimi. Since the town's main industry was based on the forests, this seems the right place for an account of Canadian forestry.

CHAPTER 6

Forestry

Here as everywhere else in Canada the most marketable forest consists
of soft or white pine. The red pine, also called Norway pine, is found
scattered around in the soft-pine forests but I was unable to determine
whether any difference in the soil caused the preponderence of one
or the other kind. The farther north, the more Norway pine, and eventually the forests of Norway pine are without rival. Norway pine grows
straighter and has a harder wood than the soft pine, but the latter is
preferred for all kinds of carpentry and is therefore in greater demand.
For coarser use, such as for beams and bridges, the Norway pine is
still used. In England, however, there is a good price for Norway pine,
so Canadian mills cut considerable quantities of Norway pine for the
English market.

The logs are from twelve to twenty feet long. The lumber is felled
mainly in the winter, but regardless of felling time, so little care is taken
to peel the bark off the trunks that the lumber left lying on the ground
is often attacked by insects and rot. By Norwegian standards the cutting
is done with little care. Logs that are less than fourteen inches in diameter are usually left behind and the lumberjack passes by any tree
that does not yield at least three logs. Forest fires are rare where the
axe has not yet done its destructive work, but where there has been
felling, the tops, branches, and twigs pave the way for fires. Consequently, a forest in which there has been logging can be considered
lost, and all the good lumber that has been carelessly left behind is
either consumed by fire or blown down by the storms that wreak
havoc among the scattered trees. I was told that fires and storms
destroyed more good forest every year than was felled for commercial
purposes. The government plans to set up new contracts for the leasing
of government forest and to stipulate that a section must be cleared

of all marketable lumber before operations are moved on to a new section. Clearly, something must be done not only to insure the government against considerable loss in revenue but to stop the steady destruction of Canada's wonderful forests.[1]

I visited two large mills owned by Mr Price and they cut about twelve hundred to fourteen hundred logs daily. The dimension was usually from twenty to forty inches and I do not believe I am far from the truth if I set the average at twenty-five inches. I never saw a log that yielded fewer than three three-by-nine-inch English planks (deals) and the yield would often be five or more. The shipments consisted mainly of deals of this dimension but there were also lots of three-by-seven-inch deals. The largest logs gave planks with a width of more than two feet. Gang saws were used here. The frames were four feet wide and set three inches apart. So boards were not cut with these saws; the enormous slabs were transported on rollers to circular saws that cut boards from the usable parts of the slabs. What was left was cut into laths and lists on still smaller circular saws. These were for use in framework walls.

What would the mill owners of Norway think of such forests and such sawmills? Would not people with a middling capital of, say, 20 to 30 thousand *speciedaler* want to acquire a prince's fortune over here?[2] The largest mills in Norway and Sweden handle hardly more than, say, four hundred and twenty logs a day, and even this yields mainly battens or two-and-a-half-by-seven-inch boards. In Canada the forest is felled mainly along the rivers and around the lakes, at most at a distance of a couple of miles; but within a decade or so it will be necessary to lay rails for horse trolleys farther into the forests to meet the annually increasing demand for lumber. I asked the consul for how long the Lake St-Jean area would be able to supply lumber at the current daily rate of one hundred and twenty dozen logs. "That will depend on the prices," he answered. There had been lumber industry on a large scale for the last fifteen or twenty years around the lake. If the prices for lumber shipments remain at the low 1863 level, the mills will concentrate on the production of high-quality, large-size lumber, and the forests will then last another six or seven years. If the prices rise to their normal level, however, the forests will probably yield lumber for twelve to fourteen years.

In the United States, government forests are sold outright. As the saying there is, the buyer has to pay cash for the forest as well as for the land before he can begin to operate. In Canada, however, the government also leases considerable stretches of forest land and later sells it with the remaining trees to settlers.[3]

I have already mentioned that the entire population of Lower Canada with the exception of some sections of the Eastern Townships is arch-French and arch-Catholic and that it is doubtful that Scandinavians would feel at home in districts where they would have to learn French and be daily witnesses to the practice of the Catholic religion. In Chicoutimi I for my part witnessed scenes and processions on roads and public places that made me feel ashamed on behalf of the local population. The Catholic bishop made a tour of the whole district, and I was told that his purpose was to bestow his blessing on the young people who had just been confirmed. In order to give him a splendid reception the inhabitants of the town had cut down enormous piles of ash trees about twenty-four feet long and set them down at six-foot intervals along both sides of the road. I counted three thousand trees and when I later discovered that this had been done everywhere I realized that entire forests were annually destroyed in order to please the bishop with greenery. Flags and streamers with Latin inscriptions were hung above the streets or waved from the houses. The procession, which travelled many miles every day, was led by dusty equestrians, riding two by two in a long row. Many of them had stringy, haggard beasts that they had decorated with an abundance of flags and multicoloured ribbons. The flags were on three-foot poles and fastened on both sides of the horses' heads. The riders were often shamefully poorly dressed but were nevertheless decorated with brilliant ribbons, and held banners with Latin inscriptions on their pommels. The overall impression was pitiable and the procession would have been more suitable as the carnival procession on the third day of the Christiania fair or as entertainment for the patients in a madhouse. Finally, behind the last decorated horse's tail, came the holy man himself, the bishop, dressed in a black cassock and riding in a four-in-hand. As he passed by, the crowds would kneel or prostrate themselves with crossed arms. The bishop stood up and made the sign of the cross to both sides. In this manner the religious leaders toured towns and countryside day after day accompanied by ridiculous buffoons to please Providence – and themselves. How could a small and isolated settlement of Lutherans feel at home with such sham!

The following day there was a magnificent political demonstration. In the recent election Mr Price had won the local seat to the Canadian Parliament. Tradition demanded that he take part in a procession all over his electoral district.[4] The procession of wagons and horses began in Chicoutimi. All the horses were decorated with flags and streamers and each wagon had banners with inscriptions like HURRAH FOR PRICE! More riders and wagons joined the procession along the way and there were frequent stops for cheers. The most commotion was made outside the home of the defeated candidate but he was hidden behind closed shutters. The procession had departed at six o'clock in the morning and did not return until six o'clock in the evening, by which time forty men rode in front of Mr Price's carriage, followed by another one hundred and fifty carriages and wagons. A stop was made in front of his home where Negro servants served refreshments. But do not think that beer and liquor were served. No, on the table there were buckets of ice water and plates of plain wheaten bread for those who wished to fortify themselves. Such a poor table after a whole day on the road suggests that the populace is unaccustomed to an abundance of food and drink.

After a few days in that hospitable home I returned to Ha! Ha! Bay on foot to have a look at the consul's property there. Time passes pleasantly for the wanderer as he converses with fields and meadows on his way. At each step he turns a page in the country's cultural history and fills the storehouse of his mind with impressions of the best original pictures, the combined efforts of nature and art. This was my experience that day. The landscape had a striking similarity to our inland districts in eastern Norway, for instance Nes in Romerike. In between the fields of clay soil there were brooklets that in the course of time had swept away the clay and created deep gutted valleys. There were fields of clover and timothy and where the fields had been neglected our common weeds seemed to thrive. The road passed through miles of firm bogland. The ditches along the road were lined with logs to keep them from collapsing. There had been attempts to cultivate the bogs and the timothy looked fine.

The consul's steward, an elderly Scotsman by the name of Mr Blair, was kind and friendly. He was also responsible for the sawmill. Conditions were not unlike those at home, where the nicely kept and rather stately homes of the stewards bear witness to the property owners' power to promote profitable as well as unprofitable enterprises. At five o'clock the next morning we sat on horseback with empty stomachs in a bitingly cold north-westerly wind to inspect the cultivated land that was said to be all of six hundred acres. This was the largest area of cultivated land free of stumps and roots that I yet had seen in Canada. There were two hundred head of cattle and a corresponding stock of horses and sheep. As in the inland part of Norway, all of this valley was exposed to drought in the spring. This year the drought had set back meadows and fields. Oats were just beginning to grow to full length on 23 July, and haying had not yet begun. The summer days were hot but not humid, as they are elsewhere in America. At night the air was cleared by northerly winds, as it is in the mountain valleys of Norway. The clayey soil does not need fertilizer for the first eight to ten years. On the land he was responsible for, Mr Blair had made use of the following rotation of crops: first year, wheat; second year, wheat; third year, oats; fourth year, hay; fifth year, hay; sixth year, hay or pasture, depending on how profitable it would be to cut the hay. He claimed that it was sufficient to plough the field to make it yield hay again. Since the soil does not get grass seed with the spreading of manure, there is no natural growth of grass and, as in Denmark, there is hardly enough growth of grass for sheep pasture after the clover and the timothy have gone. The soil gets very little fertilizer: Manure is not collected during the summer and in the winter the cattle are fed only straw, which, as you know, gives but little fertilizing power to the manure. Even though the land was better suited for rye than for wheat, winter rye was an unknown variety and spring rye was unprofitable. The steward, however, said he would try winter rye that year if he could get a supply of seed. I took the liberty of recommending our so-called "Norwegian harrow," or rotary hoe, as the best implement for the crushing of lumps of clay and the blending of fertilizer with the soil.

On this chilly morning ride I had a fine slender horse of Spanish breed. Here these horses are called "pure Canadian" but their origin can be traced back to the Spanish dominons in America. It was wonderful to be on horseback again for the first time since my arrival in America, for at home I was used to being in the saddle all the time. The consul arrived before noon and he was immediately surrounded by people who wanted to have a word with him. In the manner of constitutional monarchs in Europe he always had to have a friendly word ready for everyone in order to maintain his popularity.

Before I conclude my account of Saguenay and Lake St-Jean I must add a few observations relevant to immigration. While I have found that the soil is as productive here as in the very best agricultural districts of Norway, as demonstrated by the list of rotations given above, this part of Canada must on several counts be placed below the Eastern Townships. As long as the lumber trade lasts, the farmer will find a good market for his products. Indeed, he does not have to go farther than to the towns and villages of the Saguenay and to the lumber camps in the forests. But when the forests have been taken, agricultural products will have to be sold to the towns along the St Lawrence River and the only means of transportation to these markets are the rivers. When these are covered with ice for half the year, all communication is cut off. The Eastern Townships, on the other hand, have year-round access by railway to the sea, Quebec, and Montreal in the north and to Portland and Boston in the south.

On my return down the Saguenay I naturally saw nothing new.

When we got down to the St Lawrence the steamship kept to the northern bank all the way to the island of Orléans a few miles below Quebec. On this side the land slopes quite steeply and is covered mainly with hardwood. Wherever the land seemed arable there were fully cultivated farms. At Murray Bay we waited for four hours during the night because of the tide. Indeed, the ebb and tide are noticeable all the way up to Quebec and make this part of the St Lawrence more like a fjord than a river. The large island of Orléans was completely cultivated. The farmhouses have a great variety of design and are nice to look at as the boat passes by. All homes seem to have open porches and from these the gently sloping fields go all the way down to the water. All land on the island has long since been taken and belongs to a seigniory.

If there had been no other sign of our approaching Quebec, the conversation of the many English-speaking passengers who joined us on the last stretch of our journey would have been sufficient reminder. Everywhere almighty money was the main topic, but while the people of L'Islet, Kamouraska, Témiscouata, Rimouski, and the Saguenay Valley spoke of *piastres*, *sous*, and *ecus*, the voices here closer to Quebec called loudly for dollars, shillings, and pennies.

CHAPTER 7

A Visit to Portland in
the United States

— ∴ —

I still had not travelled in the district of the Ottawa River north and
north-west of Montreal or in the north-western part of Lower Canada
on the north side of the St Lawrence. According to all information
available to me, however, neither the climate nor the soil of these forest
lands can be compared to that of the Eastern Townships. Therefore,
I realized that I would not be able to recommend these areas to the
emigrant as long as there was better land to be had, and decided to
set aside this region for future tourists. On the other hand, the border
states of Maine, Vermont, and New Hampshire in the United States
and the British Province of New Brunswick seemed of greater potential
interest to the emigrant. All of these states are actively encouraging
the stream of emigration to flow across their borders. In Canada petty
nationalism stood in the way of acquiring information – or perhaps
it was merely inefficiency. Faithful to my plan of not writing down
anything of significance that was not based on my own experience,
I decided to make this little detour before I left Lower Canada behind.

When I arrived in Quebec from Saguenay before noon on 24 July
the indefatigable Buchanan informed me that the Commissioner of
Crown Lands wished to see me. I immediately went to the ministry,
and the secretary, Mr Russell,[1] introduced me to the minister,
Mr McDougall, a tall and slim young man with the stamp of the lawyer
on his features.[2] Our conversation naturally centered on Scandinavian
emigration. In Norway I could have received indirect subsidy for the
considerable expenses involved in my rather ambitious undertaking
of travelling throughout North America and having my observations
and experiences published, if I only would commit myself, as one
Norwegian cabinet minister expressed it, to writing a book that would
serve the government; that is, scare the Norwegian people from
emigrating. Later I was offered agencies by land companies in the

United States to entice emigrants to their land, and now this Canadian minister quite unabashedly suggested that if I were to commit myself to a favourable report on Canada I could expect the support of his government. In one respect, however, Mr McDougall proved himself more magnanimous than these others; for when I declared that the purpose of my journey would have been entirely wasted if I were to enter the service of any party, and when I firmly insisted that I planned to publish my negative observations as well as my positive ones, he nevertheless encouraged me to continue my investigations and gave me some subsidy without requesting any kind of return favour.

Thereafter I was taken up to the Forestry Department where I looked at a very nice collection of Canadian trees. They told me that the present Lieutenant Colonel Kierulf[3] from Norway had visited Canada some years earlier and inspected this collection. I then looked up my friendly countryman, Mr Anderson,[4] then employed in Mr Buchanan's office, and asked him to keep my books, bed, and bedding for me since I would have no further use for them until I returned to Norway later in the fall, as was then my plan. At four o'clock that same afternoon I was on the train to Portland. Haying had still not begun in the fields between Quebec and Richmond, but farther south the hay was in stacks. Haying had started a week earlier in the Eastern Townships, still more evidence of the beneficial climate of this area compared to the rest of Lower Canada.

I had been told so many stories of the deceitful Yankees and their dexterity in getting into other people's pockets that I was more careful than usual after we had passed the border station of Island Pond. My own attitude reminded me of the Christiania manufacturers I had had the honour and the worry of guiding on their visit to London in 1862. They were so frightened of the many stories they had heard of murderers and pickpockets that they walked around their first day in London adhering to the motto, "The right hand on the pocketbook and the left on the heart." Had not my own pocketbook been so empty and my heart so worthless I would have had good reason for equal anxiety.

In all railway stations there were posters with the brief but eloquent legend: BEWARE OF PICKPOCKETS! I never saw any of these knights of industry but observed many involved in other confidence traffic on the train, charming young women whose trade took them to and from the towns on the Atlantic coast. In the summer season they stayed at hotels in the mountains of Vermont and Maine and made frequent journeys on the trains to capture travellers who were blessed with an abundance of vitality and a bottomless pocketbook. Paupers like myself had nothing to fear from them, nor anything to hope for.

There is, however, another source of irritation that I had come across sporadically in Canada but that I disvovered was a way of life on this excursion to the Great Republic: the immodesty of young people.[5] I can remember that when Professor Welhaven[6] discussed the definition of modesty, he insisted that the word was empty of meaning for youth since it was only the mature man who had acquired sufficient material and spiritual greatness to have anything worth relinquishing: Thus he alone could demonstrate modesty. Youth, on the other hand, had no experience of life, no capital to relinquish, and consequently had neither the qualifications nor the obligation to have this virtue. As students we were puzzled by this manner of talk, for when we as children had been taught to write, one of the first printed exercises we had had to copy had been: "Modesty is the most pleasing virtue a youth can have." In the United States, however, Professor Welhaven would have had great success with his theory since American youth is as a rule entirely without modesty. They demand and take the best wherever they have a chance. In railway coaches, on steamships, and in public gatherings they press forward and take the best seats without any respect for age, and in conversation their opinions are the first and the best even though they cannot base them on either knowledge or insight. Gradually the European realizes that civilized deportment is not regarded with respect but, on the contrary, is misunderstood as a sign of weakness. If he wants to get anywhere he had better make himself respected wherever he can, and be the first to get his hands on the dish and to place his feet on tables or benches. Old emigrants will be able to verify that they have had to struggle tooth and nail in order to get their contractual rights, for the Yankee will coldly turn his back on modest behaviour. If he realizes, however, that he is dealing with people who look out for themselves, he can be the best man to do business with.

It is only a hundred and twenty-five miles from the Eastern Townships through the States down to Portland and the landscape was for the most part mountainous, with rivers running through gently sloping valleys. There were some stretches of moor and flat plains with woods in between. Most of the soil should be classified as third class. It was either mixed with sand or the layer of topsoil in the forest had sand underneath. The summer climate, however, is favourable. Corn thrived in the fields and there were magnificent orchards, mainly of apple trees. If a settler has the necessary capital to clear the forest, the land here of course has as many advantages for the farmer as the best land in Canada since the orchards give such good profits. But since it must be a basic assumption that the emigrant arrives without capital, this book should not be concerned with an evaluation of the potential qualities of the land but consider what the poor emigrant may be able to achieve without great cost. The considerable expenses involved in clearing land are thus an effective barrier between the poor and the best forest land, while poor soil with a poor but natural growth of grass will yield quicker results. And the emigrant has no time for patient waiting. Much has been done to entice the Scandinavians to Maine. Indeed, one of the governors of the state did so much to get Norwegians to settle here that he was called "the Norwegian governor."[7] But these attempts failed.

At a later date I had the opportunity to travel through several of the north-eastern states. The available land is almost always covered with forest. The landscape has great beauty. In particular the valley of the Androscoggin River in New Hamsphire is like a Garden of Eden. Orchards came down to the banks of the river and behind them fields and meadows stretched to sides of mountains with tops that were always covered in mist when I was there. The valley presented a living image of the *watercolor drawings* so favoured by the English.[8] I have never seen a more beautiful landscape in America. The vegetation in Maine and New Hampshire is much like that of the Eastern Townships. In mountainous Vermont, however, it is poorer. The summer temperatures are not so extreme because of the vicinity of the sea, but the winters are very harsh. I saw two-and-a-half-foot-thick ice from a nearby lake brought to houses in Portland.

In Portland I met several Norwegians, among them Mr Johnsen, a woodcarver from Chicago, and Mr Zimmermann, who now sought his living as a carpenter after having failed in his attempts to clear land in the Eastern Townships. "Bury," he observed, "is the ruin of all. The grain is without kernel and the haying is made difficult by all the stumps and rocks that not only took up space but made it difficult to get at the grass with the scythe. Weeds were always threatening to crowd out cultivated plants and the winters are terrible with their snow and extreme cold." This prejudiced account led me to ask him the following questions:

Q: Did you take the proximity of the tall forest into consideration and take care not to sow closer than a hundred feet from the trees? For soil close to trees will always yield straw but little or no kernel.
A: Neither I nor the others thought of this. We sowed close up to the edge of the forest.
Q: Did you take care to place each variety of seed in the soil by the date given to ensure against frost before harvest time?
A: We could not burn the felled trees until the wood was sufficiently dry, and after the fire we sowed in the ashes. In this way the seed was often

sown rather late and the harvest was ruined if we had frost in September.

Q: Frost in September may occur anywhere in the northern parts of North America; but if you had sown earlier, the grain would have been ready for harvest in August.

A: But I knew a man who fertilized his clearing with cow manure and then sowed wheat. In spite of all this work he got very little wheat, while the worthless straw grew to an exceptional height.

Q: If a naturally rich soil is fertilized, it will in all countries yield a rich harvest of straw but very little grain. The soil in Bury or elsewhere in Canada is no exception to this rule. Had you any agricultural experience before you tried farming in Canada?

A: No.

This is the story of many emigrants. They set out to do in America things they have never attempted at home, and when they fail in their endeavours they blame the land rather than their own lack of experience and their own mistakes.

My original plan had been to go by sea from Portland to New Brunswick, but since the steamship was not scheduled for departure for another week and this trip would consequently have taken at least half a month of my time, I had to give up this journey in order to get to Upper Canada in time for the wheat harvest. New Brunswick, moreover, is all forest land of the same general quality as in Lower Canada.

On my return to Richmond I met countrymen who told me that even though they were doing well in Canada they had nevertheless decided to go farther west into the States because in Canada they had to live without hearing the word of God. It has often seemed strange to me that Norwegian mission associations spend so many thousands on the questionable conversion of heathens in Africa instead of looking after the spiritual needs of their own kin in America. The English give priority to their countrymen and provide them with churches and clergy, and I cannot understand what has led honourable Norwegian men and women not to take on such a natural responsibility. Providence has given all of us nations to which we belong and to which we should give our first allegiance.

I have already described the landscape we travelled through to Montreal. On the large prairie on this side of Montreal some of the fields of barley had begun to turn yellow, but most were green as grass, as were the oat fields. In Montreal I met Captain Svanøe from Bergen.[9] He had just brought a load of emigrants from Norway. As a man experienced in this traffic he complained of all the trouble poor emigrants caused for the ships' captains. On arriving in Quebec the emigrant will frequently not have a single shilling; nor will he have the slightest notion of how to travel farther or how to acquire provisions. His destitution leads to suffering and illness and there is no authority with any responsibility for his welfare. The surest and easiest method to change this sad state of affairs, which brings shame on our entire nation, is in the hands of the Norwegian authorities, had they only the will to make use of it. We have all kinds of laws regulating the fitting out of emigrant ships and the ratio of emigrants according to tonnage. Could we not add a regulation that no ship may take on emigrants who cannot show evidence of sufficient funds for further travel in America, say $15 a person? The implementation of such a law would save many Norwegian emigrants from suffering and even death. If the Norwegian government had been aware of the difficulties and suffering of the poor among the numerous Norwegian emigrants in 1866, had they witnessed their helplessness when in droves of several hundreds they would lie like beggars in the streets in the raw night air, then they would perhaps have paid attention to this piece of advice.

CHAPTER 8

Canada West or Upper Canada

The mighty Ottawa River, which flows from the north, marks the division between Upper and Lower Canada. Towards the west the land extends in an almost two-hundred-mile long peninsula that has the Great Lakes on three sides. This peninsula is situated between forty-two and forty-five degrees north latitude; Thus, the most southerly parts of Lower Canada are not farther south than the most northern part of this peninsula. Nevertheless, neither this peninsula nor any other part of Canada West has higher summer or lower winter temperatures than Canada East. The main difference between them is that spring may come a little earlier and the fall a little later in Upper Canada. All of Upper Canada is forest land and the numerous farms cultivated in the English style were originally a wilderness of virgin forest with first- and second-class soil. When Upper Canada is hailed now as a far more fertile and productive land than the rest of Canada, the reason in my view is not that the soil is more fertile than in other parts of Canada but that the easy communication provided by the Great Lakes has led people with capital to invest it in agriculture here. Considerable areas are therefore under the plough now and the annual export of wheat from Canada West is quite significant.

It would thus be wrong to advise the emigrant to choose Upper Canada rather than Lower Canada. The labour involved in clearing land is the same and the settler is exposed to the same problems and the same difficulties during the first years. Moreover, the building of the Grand Trunk Railroad through all of Canada has meant that it now matters little where you settle as long as the distance to the market and to the railroad is reasonable. This view of the advantages of western Canada is apparently different from that of most other travellers, but the reader will have to judge for himself on the basis of my experiences.

From Montreal I continued my journey along the St Lawrence to its source at the outlet of Lake Ontario at Kingston, a distance of about a hundred and fifty miles. In all counties north of the railroad there is available forest land. All crops in the area through which I travelled were doing poorly on the old fields. This was partly due to the drought, but the main reason was the exhaustion of the soil after many years of use without fertilizing. Therefore the soil should not always be evaluated by its yield since the systematic soil exhaustion so common in North America and particularly in the West will sooner or later impoverish even the best naturally rich soil. Nor should one confuse any classification of the soil here with our notions of good or bad agricultural land in Norway, for what I refer to as poor soil here in America is the equal to the best soil in Norway and to the natural soil of the most fertile parts of Denmark.

The land to the west of Kingston was owned by people of some means. Agriculture was well organized and the crops stood high all the way to Toronto, about a hundred and sixty miles from Kingston. At three junctions along the way there are railroads that go north.[1] The well-known Canadian author, Mrs Traill, whose letters on Canada are read with great interest in Europe, has settled in Peterborough County halfway between Kingston and Toronto.[2] Her publications have led many younger members of English families to settle in this area. Toronto is famous for its beautiful setting. It has the appearance of having been projected in a forest of gigantic hardwoods where the only trees felled were those in the way of streets, buildings, and gardens. The citizens of Toronto have understood the art of bringing the country into the city. Here youth does not need to *ride summer by*[3] since summer covers the buildings with its umbrageous foliage. Below the town is Lake Ontario where steamships ceaselessly go back and forth with grain and meat from the West, and at the docks lumber rafts are formed for the passage down the St Lawrence.

In Peterborough and Victoria counties the Canadian Land and Emigration Company has areas totalling two hundred and fifty thousand acres for sale.[4] All of it is forest land and riddled with small rivers and lakes. Since I could see no reason why the emigrant should pay $4.00 or $5.00 an acre for that land when he could just as conveniently buy government land that was just as good for from 25 cents to $1.00; and since this Company land had no advantages, such as completed buildings or clearings, compared to government land, I turned down an offer from the director, Mr Frederic T. Roche, to explore the Company's land with their engineer and decided to go from Toronto to government land.[5] The land between Toronto and Lake Simcoe had both evergreen and hardwood forests. The fields were well kept and the wheat harvest had begun. The soil consisted of a porous, greyish mould with some clay. The potatoes were ready for eating.

On 28 July I boarded the steamboat that would take us across the thirty-mile-long Lake Simcoe to the village of Orillia,[6] where one of the government agents had his quarters. The shores of Lake Simcoe were flat and wooded. There were very few clearings since the land had been bought by speculators and thus was shunned by emigrants as long as they could purchase more advantageous government land elsewhere. Winters here are as cold as they are in Norway and the summers as warm, but spring and fall combine to give the farmer almost a couple of months more than in eastern Norway. On the southern shores of Lake Couchiching, a continuation of Lake Simcoe, is the delightful village of Orillia with hardwood forests in the background, beautiful gardens in its midst, and charming islands in the foreground. It was a Danish lake with Danish shores where the trees stood on the beach and the leaves kissed the water. No wonder that the merry young people of Toronto liked to spend their summers there. Small rowboats and sailboats had been brought up to Lake Simcoe by rail and every day pleasure boats filled with ladies and gentlemen could be seen passing the village.

Since the government agent, Mr Oliver,[7] was busy with his monthly accounts – as an American husband he also had to take on many of those duties which in Europe are taken care of by the wife – and since in addition to taking care of everything in the household he also had a cow in calf in his stable, I could appreciate that this busy man desired to have a few extra days before we set out on a long and strenuous excursion in the woods. In the meantime I had time to explore the country around Lake Couchiching and to enjoy the pleasant company of the vacationers in Orillia.

To begin with, I balked at the heavy breakfast so common in America.[8] Steak and ham can hardly be considered a light diet, but now it all goes down fairly easily. At first I also followed the Norwegian custom and spent sufficient time at the table to allow the food to be masticated before it left the mouth, but I soon got used to shovelling in whatever was at arm's length as if I were alone at the table and as if I were always in a hurry to catch a train. The American will burp without embarrassment at the table and it can truly be an unappetizing experience to sit close to people who for their own convenience let go of one chest f--t after the other. No one waits until the others are finished: You get up and leave the gluttony (the word that best describes the American dining-room) whenever you feel so inclined.

On one of my morning excursions I arrived at a farm a few miles from Orillia where an educated and extremely polite man was living and trying to farm. Basil Rowe's farm was about a hundred acres, of which seventy-five were cultivated. The maple did not yield as much as in eastern Canada, he told me, and it should not be counted on for an extra income. In his experience Canada was a good country for the poor but not a good place for the gentleman farmer to make a living. The only exceptions were the large farms in the West. The farms here were usually too small and the day wages too high for the owner to make a profit when hired help were used. Such was his story. The wheat harvest was also unpredictable. The year before, he had harvested twenty bushels per acre, but now he showed me fields from which he could hardly expect more than seven to eight bushels per acre. They had been devastated by midge, a frequent scourge in Canada as well as in the United States. Some say they come from the East, others say from the West, but the most reasonable explanation is that they attack land that is nearly exhausted while they pass by new or well-preserved land. Since the land is always used until it is exhausted, the midge will appear everywhere, inflicting revenge for the misdeeds of the past.[9] In this part of the country the cattle are usually put out to pasture around 8 May and stabled for winter late in November, so the farm animals can fend for themselves for almost seven months. The winters were rather cold. On the surrounding lakes the ice was from eighteen to thirty-six inches thick in the winter. On another farm where a settler had an eight-acre lot of potatoes, wheat, and corn, the corn had been damaged by frost early in July. The plants still had yellowish leaves after the frost but otherwise seemed to have survived the ordeal and had the appearance of a normal yield. Frost nights can occur even in the middle of summer but the forests are hardly to blame for this irregular climate: From the wide ice-strewn spaces of Hudson Bay northerly winds carry unexpected frosts into the prairies of Illinois as well as into the forests of Canada. Land held by speculators cost from $6.00 to $10 an acre.

Directly across the lake from Orillia there is an Indian reservation where the band of the Ojibwa tribe now lives that used to own Orillia but from which they had to withdraw on the white man's arrival.[10] I crossed the lake in a canoe with an Indian paddler and visited the Indian town of Rama, which had three hundred and fifty inhabitants. After having spent a couple of hours in pleasant conversation with their friendly missionary I walked around the village.[11] The dwellings were log cabins but nothing could grow on the barren sands they had been given to live on, so they had neither trees, potatoes, nor grain. There were a few old Indians present who could still remember the times when the pale-faces had not yet arrived in Toronto and when the Ojibwa tribe ruled most of Canada. The Ojibwas are not a beautiful race. Their faces are wide and flat and their heads are shaped like turnips. They do not have the aggressive features of the Sioux and other horseriding tribes in the West. The Ojibwas are called canoe Indians by the Indians of the West to distinguish them from the horseback Indians on the western plains.

Wives and young girls were busy outdoors sewing canoes. They sat eight to a canoe, four on either side, and sewed with long wooden needles. The ninth took care of the coffee pot and they all talked at once, but for a white man it was impossible to get as much as a word or a look from any of them. On our way back there were four of us in the canoe; one was a young squaw. She dutifully turned her back on me. The two Indians paddled along the shore and the islands, for their tradition is never to paddle right across a lake but to keep to the shore as much as possible. Halfway we had to stop at an island because the canoe took in more water than the young squaw could bail out. We emptied the canoe and laid branches and leaves in the bottom and so I could again stretch out my legs and contemplate the lovely shores as well as other canoes on the lake on their way to Orillia, where the steamboat the *Fairy* was to depart that evening on a moonlight excursion out on Lake Simcoe.

This excursion and a concert to be held that same evening were organized to collect money for a church for which the building costs had exceeded the budget. At the concert the amateur singers had to strike "Ave Maria" from their program as an unsuitable song for such an occasion, while, in the service of the same cause, music and dancing aboard the boat were found suitable. At least one-third of the passengers on the cruise were Indians, who looked strangely artificial in civilized dress. Fashionable straw hats with flowers and feathers did not belong pressed down on the yellowish-brown foreheads of the Indian women. Nor did they look becoming in crinolines and other finery. I find that these children of the forest look much better in the natural dress of their own choice. Dressed up in the white man's clothes the Indians, and especially the women, look like characters at a masquerade. With lively dancing to poor music, both sadly out of harmony with the solemn panorama that glided past us in the moonlight, we made a wide circle out on the lake. When the excursion was over, however, it was difficult to see whether the passengers had had fun or not, since the American party face does not express wanton joy but is fixed in an expression between laughing and crying.

The agent was now ready for a tour of the forests and when the magic flute was heard from the steamboat at dawn we hurried aboard and cast out our fishing lines to catch black bass. After we had gone about fifteen miles we went ashore at the northern end of Lake Couchiching where there was a little sawmill. There we entered a

common farm wagon outfitted with extraordinarily big wheels to mini-
mize the jolts on the worst forest road I have ever seen in America.[12]
Our transport also served as mail carrier and brought small packages
of flour and other goods to the settlers many miles farther north. The
road to Lake Muskoka went through a rocky landscape with forests
of evergreens as well as hardwood. Oak, which I had not seen in eastern Canada, was frequent but I would have had to go farther south
into the States to find hickory. The evergreens stood tall but this forest
had no current commercial value. The settlers had a hard time cutting
it down and burning the trunks to make way for fields and meadows.
The valley widened to a broad plain as we approached Lake Muskoka,
but this flat land had already been taken by speculators. In Gravenhurst,
a settlement of Germans, tobacco was being grown according to
German custom.[13] The seed could not be sown in the open,
however, and the plants were first grown along with cabbage plants
in a cold frame and replanted later. Their log cabins were miserable,
as they were in all new settlements. The buildings the Norwegians had
abandoned in Bury were like villas compared to these. Winter wheat
was now being cut but the summer wheat and the oats were still green
the first days of August. Turnips and potatoes thrived in between the
stumps. In this manner we continued apace along the road, crossing
mile-long stretches of corduroy roads, low rocky ridges, and forest-
clad plains. No log used on the road was less than eighteen inches
in diameter.

We passed through the townships of North Orillia, Norrison, and
Muskoka. The government had not yet surveyed most of the land
around Lake Muskoka. Only a few squatters had begun their pioneer
work. There were also some Yankees who had fled from conscription
in the States and who now spent their time fishing and hunting. The
lake had many islands as yet unsettled, but they were strewn with rocks
and clearing them would have meant a lot of work. The squatters,
however, had been quite active in this area. Frequently they had
merely cut down a few trees along the lakeshore or river bank so that
they could claim the land when the government was ready to sell.
On one claim the only so-called "improvement" had been to cut
crosses on the tree trunks. They speculated on being able to sell their
claims to settlers who then would have to pay the squatters for their
claim before paying the government for the actual land. At the mouth
of the Muskoka River, for instance, there were three handsome young
men, the Browning brothers, who had had to pay off a squatter with
$1,200.

We sailed into the mouth of the Muskoka River where we visited
an English gentleman, Mr Alport.[14] In him I met one of these living

mysteries who with money in his pocket had left the country of his birth to clear a large estate in the Canadian wilderness. He had the forest cut down and burnt and he built and organized as if his pocket-book had an endless supply. His main aim was to get some future interest on the money he had spent. He had buried his capital in the land and did not expect to be able to retrieve it, and in this he was surely not mistaken. From his hospitable home we continued farther up the Muskoka River to the waterfalls where there were vague plans to establish a town. A French Canadian with Indian blood in his veins had settled here. He had an extensive trade with the Indians and belonged to the class of courageous traders so well described by Cooper and other novelists.[15]

There was even a hotel of sorts that served fried pork in the morning and boiled pork for dinner. For supper there was cold pork for the sake of variety. We went up a ladder through a hole in the ceiling to the dormitory where the windows were without panes and covered with sheets as protection against the insects and the wind. The floor, however, was well appointed, for even though the loose planks were placed so far apart that a leg could easily find its way through the cracks, a fine carpet was spread over it all and thus disguised these flaws in the carpentry work. At dawn I woke up at the sound of a shot outside. I thought someone was shooting wild pigeons for break-fast, turned over, and was soon fast asleep again. Half an hour later there was another shot, but I paid as little attention to it as to the first one. But after a while Mr Oliver came up the ladder and informed me that they had called twice for breakfast and I would now have to eat alone since the main meal service was over. I was well aware that in America one is called, rung, blown, gong-gonged, or drummed to a meal but how was I to know that one could also be summoned to breakfast by a shot? The hotel had not yet been able to acquire the more common instruments of sound and therefore they had settled on a rifle to call people to their meals.[16]

We walked on foot up towards Parry Sound and the Magnetawan River. The days were hot and humid and we were rather uncomfort-able. I was never exposed to baked pigeons flying into my mouth in America.[17] but the mosquitoes made such massed attacks on our eyes, ears, and mouths that we were constantly beating about our heads with twigs. These flying devils bit me so much that blood streamed down my neck, and some time later when I looked at myself in a mirror in Chicago I looked as if I had had the pox. We now came across fewer and fewer clearings and eventually all signs of civiliza-tion were left behind. A few squatters may have set up their log cabins along the shores of Georgian Bay, but the territory around the mighty

Magnetawan River was yet untouched by the axe. Only occasional beaver trappers or deer hunters, whose canoes we passed, wandered freely around in the forests.

Canada West has placed its hopes for the future in the land between Toronto and Georgian Bay, where Parry Sound has all the appearance of becoming an important place. There is some talk of building canals from this point to connect the inland districts with the maritime traffic on the Great Lakes, with the States to the west, and with Toronto to the south. At least half of these vast areas are covered with evergreen forest, the rest with hardwood. In the country along the Magnetawan birch is dominant, then sugar maple and pine, all of which are found growing in the same forest. The reader should be able to evaluate the soil on the basis of this information. As soon as the necessary means of transportation have been established, the enormous evergreen forests will yield lumber for many years and bring capital and industry to the internal regions. But in the years before this development can take place the settler will in my view have to live a slave's life. Most of the clearings I saw were in evergreen forest and the only comfort for the settler would be ignorance of any better land or any easier way to make a living. I would not hesitate to recommend the best parts of Canada East before this section of Canada West, where the farmer's products are always in competition with those from the States and where the prices reflect the costs of the long transportation to the markets and ports of the East.

In order to let the reader see the costs involved in pioneering in the forests of this part of Canada and to make him better informed about the chores of the settler, I will first make a list of some basic figures and then present some of the facts of the daily life of the pioneer farmer in the form of an abbreviated diary.

NECESSITIES FOR SETTLING ON FOREST LAND

Victuals for one year (based on the needs of a family of husband, wife, and three small children):

8 barrels of flour	$50.00
2 barrels of pork at 196 lbs each	$15.00
80 bushels of potatoes	$50.00
30 lbs of tea	$20.00
1 barrel of herring	$10.00
½ barrel of salt	$2.00

```
Seed:
20 bushels of potatoes          $10.00
 3 bushels of wheat              $6.00
10 bushels of oats               $5.00
                                _____
                                $168.00
```

Other necessities: 1 axe $2; 1 grindstone $2; 1 shovel $1; 2 hoes $2; 1 scythe $1; 2 drills $3; 1 handsaw $2; 2 water buckets $1; 1 paned window with frame $2; 1 baking oven $1; 2 pots $2.50; 1 kettle $1; 1 frying pan $1; 1 teapot $0.50; 6 tin cups $0.50; 3 large tin platters $2; 6 spoons $0.25; 6 knives and forks $1; 3 sets of woollen blankets $20; 2 quilted bedspreads $1.50; 2 sets of sheets $1.50; 1 flat-iron $0.75; 1 pig $4; 1 cow $25; hay for the first year $15. Total: $93.50.

All of this roughly adds up to approximately $260. Usually the settler will not need a plough or a harrow his first year.

A SETTLER'S DIARY

April 10. Arrived at my log cabin in the clearing after driving 40 miles across rough country. It took me 2 days since driving was made difficult by the still-frostbound ground. I placed my apple trees in a hole in my future garden, fed my horses and oxen, and made myself a good cup of tea. This was my first day as a settler.

April 11. My hired hand, Hans, watered horses and cattle and as it was Sunday we went to meeting in the morning and afternoon.

April 12. Scolded Hans for having been out so late last night; planted apple and plum trees; worked on the fence; opened the pork barrel and found that it was unspoiled; broke the spout of the teapot; borrowed a frying pan; and boiled some potatoes in a copper, having forgotten to provide my home with the necessary utensils. 2 cows calved and a sheep gave birth to 2 lambs.

April 13. Began to plow for wheat. Hired a man for $20 per month plus meals for the summer. Another cow calved.

April 14. Hired a cook for $4 per month. Karl is setting up fences; Hans is still ploughing with the oxen; I worked in the garden, sowing onions, beets, lettuce, etc. Bought 4 cows at $18 each.

April 15. Sowed wheat after having swollen the seed in salt water and dried it in lime. As is common here, 3½ acres took 4 bushels of seed. Sowed peas and other early garden vegetables. Hans is still ploughing. 2 sheep had lambs.

April 16. Ploughed for the first time for potatoes and corn.

April 17. Continued this work for the rest of the month and sowed 4 acres with a mixture of oats and peas.

May 1. All worked on the road.

May 2. All attended meeting.

May 3. One of the men churned butter before breakfast; cut wood for the kitchen; too hot for ploughing with oxen in the middle of the day, so we all worked on the fences.

May 4–5. It rained both days; made 2 new rakes; sharpened and made handles for the new axes; repairs in the barn.

May 6. Weather is nice, but still too wet for the plough, so we all worked on the fence. Hans off to the mill with some oats to get us a little flour.

May 7. Hot and humid; ploughed for corn from daybreak till 10 in the morning and from 4 in the afternoon till dark. Cleared stones off the cornfield; completed the garden; fetched the oatmeal.

May 8. A neighbour killed by a tree that fell on him. Same work as yesterday morning; then the neighbours helped us to raise a log barn 40 ft. long and 30 ft. wide.

May 9. All at meeting. We never fail to listen to the word of God on Sundays. A heavy thunderstorm.

May 10. Carted manure to the cornfield and ploughed it into the soil, etc.

May 12–13. Same work; sowed corn and pumpkin; went to the neighbour's burial.

May 14–15. Sowed more oats; completed sowing of corn; killed a calf and sold a quarter for $1.25.

May 16. Sunday.

May 17. Spent the rest of the month completing an old clearing; hauled lumber with the oxen; sheared sheep on a rainy day (the sheep had been sheltered before it began to rain); began to sow corn in the new clearing.

June 1–2. Sowed oats on 1½ acres cleared land; Hans ploughed the potato field for the second time; Karl carted and spread manure in front of the plough; I followed him with the seed potatoes. It should be noted that it is impossible to sow in straight rows as long as the stumps and roots are in the ground.

June 3. The potatoes are done. This year sowing has been as follows: wheat 3½ acres; peas 3 acres; oats 5 acres; corn 6 acres; potatoes 5½ acres; all in all 23 acres. In addition there are 20 acres of meadow, 13 of oats, and 20 that have been partly cleared. The total is then 76 acres.

June 4–15. The new fences are completed and the old ones fixed; a road built across a small bog on my land; set up a small house at the bottom of the garden, a house not found on many properties in this area but which people with some sense of decency cannot do without.

June 16 to the end of the month. Ridged corn and potatoes; extremely
   hot, the thermometer at 86° Fahrenheit on some days; sowed 1 acre
   of turnip in the new clearing.
July 1–3. Ridged corn for the second time.
July 5. Rain. Sharpened scythes.
July 6. Began haying.
July 15. Completed haying without having had a single drop of rain
   on the hay; very hot.
July 16. Heavy storm with thunder and lightning. A barn burnt down
   on a neighbouring farm because a labourer entered with a lighted
   pipe. It is difficult to remove the pipe from the mouth of a Canadian
   labourer. Killed a fat calf.
July 17. All hay in stacks.
July 18. Sunday. Weather cold, as always after a thunderstorm.
July 19. Began to ridge corn for the third time or, rather, to clear away
   the weeds that had come up since the second time; sold 200 lbs
   butter at 17 cents per lb; cut the first cucumber in my garden.
July 20 to the end of the month. Completed ridging of corn and potatoes; began clearing new land by cutting away the underbrush and
   placing it in piles ready for burning. For the rest of the summer this
   work continued on 30 acres as often as time could be set aside. In
   the winter large trees are felled and cut up in pieces to be piled and
   burned. The summer is best for clearing land since the foliage, when
   dry, makes it easier to burn the trees.
August 2. Attended a meeting to discuss the building of a church tower;
   cleared underbrush; the first potatoes of the season.
August 4–30. Cleared more land for winter wheat up to the 10th, when
   we began to cut grain. By the 21st all had been harvested with the
   exception of a quarter-acre of late oats and corn. The first melon
   on our table.
August 31. Began to clear land again. Killed a lamb.
September 1–10. Same work and sowed 3 acres of winter wheat; began
   to make potash of the wood that had been burned.
September 11–22. Worked in the underbrush; made more potash until
   I had 2 full barrels, which I sold for $60. The neighbour's cattle
   broke into my cornfield but did not do much damage.
September 23. Rain; threshing and cleaning of 1½ bushels of wheat
   and 8 bushels of oats; sent it to the mill; the oats weighed 48 lbs.
September 24. Made a wooden box for steaming; it can take 12 bushels.
September 25. Began fall ploughing; a dry cow set on a fattening diet
   for killing. A neighbour lost an ox that had broken into my cornfield
   and eaten too much green corn. This should encourage him to
   fix his part of the fence, something I have not yet been able to

persuade him to do.

September 27. Began steaming pumpkins for the pigs that now are set on a fattening diet; threshed 5 bushels of peas and oats and had them ground for mixing with the pumpkins (a few weeks in advance I had given the pigs uncooked feed); hollowed out a pine log for a trough; went on a squirrel hunt that should be more fully explained: When there is a rich harvest of nuts in the forest the squirrels arrive in such numbers that they devastate the cornfields. Neighbours then set a date for a hunt for squirrels and other animals that do damage to the farmer. All members of the male sex, young and old, then gather at the appointed meeting place and split up in two teams, each with an elected leader. The team that shoots fewer animals than the other will have to organize and pay for a ball for the entire party at the closest village hotel. Each animal is valued according to its harmfulness by a point system. Thus the right forepaw of a bear will count for 400 points; a raccoon 100; a squirrel, crow, or woodpecker 1 each; etc. At dawn eager hunters swarm the woods and in the afternoon women and children swarm the clearings bringing refreshments to the men. No work is done on the farms and the beds stand empty at night since this is the best time to hunt bears and raccoons, which give the most points. We carry on like this for three wonderful days and nights. Then the bounty is brought to the village where a referee is elected to decide which team is the winner. The team I belonged to had two bears = 800, 4 raccoons = 400, 473 squirrels, 27 crows, and 105 wood-peckers, altogether 1,805 points. Even so, we lost, since the other team had one bear more than we did.

September 29–30. Hans is ploughing and Karl and I are harvesting corn. In the afternoon there was a husking bee to help us get the work done.

October 1–2. The same work; in the afternoon a husking bee at one of the neighbouring farms.

October 4–11. Ploughing; husking completed; the cornstalks cut up and piled; pumpkins and onions harvested.

October 12. Stacked the corn stalks; set up a fence around these and the haystacks.

October 13. Began to harvest potatoes.

October 14–30. Potato harvest completed – 800 bushels; potato fields ploughed; land cleared. Hired Karl for the winter at $7 a month.

October 22. The sun is shining on the trees that have taken on autumn colours. The maples are dark red, the aspen and beech trees golden, and the walnut trees brown; but the brave oak still defies the season and stands alone dark green in the multicoloured forest.

November 1. The same work continues; turnips, cabbage, and other garden produce are harvested. (350 bushels of turnips.) The cows are stabled for the night.

November 2. First real frost. Ploughing had to wait till the afternoon. Land cleared

November 3–20. Cleared underbrush; cut firewood; Cows stabled for the night; heavy frost; no more ploughing.

November 21. First snow; all animals stabled.

November 22. Thaw and rain; more grain threshed for the pigs.

November 23–30. One day of ploughing; killed 1 lamb; heavy frost but beautiful weather. Indian summer.

December 1–4. More Indian summer; wood cutting and clearing.

December 5. Butchered pigs.

December 6. Snow; threshing; cut up the pork and salted it in barrels.

December 7. Hauled firewood since there was not enough snow for the sled.

December 8–9. Made a sled for the oxen; cut firewood.

December 10–11. Brought home firewood on the sled.

December 13. Snowstorm; threshing.

December 14. Took home a load of corn stalks. I cannot take hay from the barn since it is still covered with the grain. I will not touch the haystacks until I can take it all into the barn.

December 15. Began to fell and cut up the tall trees on the land I had cleared of underbrush; cut and sledded firewood; cut and split fence rails; drove logs for a new barn; threshed; looked after the animals; skidded logs of hemlock and then drove them to the sawmill to make boards for the new barn; drove a few logs home to make shingles for the roof; went to town with butter and a little grain and brought home a few necessities. The winter was passed with such chores.

The next spring the snow was on the ground till April 20, but after that everything grew quickly and with great intensity.

SEASONS FOR SOWING AND HARVESTING

On forest land the snow usually melts during the first half of April and the land can be ploughed between 25 April and 1 May.

Peas can be sowed until 20 May; also corn; spring wheat until 25 May; Swedish turnips or rutabaga until 15 May; oats until 1 June; potatoes until 24 June; cabbage seed sown in cold frames around 15 April and replanted around 1 June.

Haying usually begins around 12 July. One man can cut about one and a quarter acres of grass a day. The hay is usually stacked in the fields.

Fall wheat is ready for harvest around 1 August. Spring wheat is ready around 10 August. Oats may be cut around 14 August. The peas can be taken around 5 August. Corn is harvested around 8 September. Four men are needed to harvest one acre a day. Women and children can do almost the same amount of work. The potato harvest will depend on the time of seeding.

All harvesting is usually done by 10 October. Then one can concentrate on clearing land. Potash is made and winter clothes are mended. The ashes of about two and a half acres of hardwood yield one barrel of second-grade potash, which may be sold for $30. The pans and coolers for this industry cost about $56, but they may be had on account with the merchant, who will take payment in potash.

In my description of Canada I have gone into considerable detail about its agriculture. This has been done deliberately so that unnecessary repetitions can be avoided in my later chapter on cultivating forest land in the United States. The forest belt of Canada stretches on through several of the north-western states. Wherever the settler decides to pioneer on this kind of land, the conditions are roughly the same regardless of the political authority by which the land is controlled. The reader can thus regard the chapter on farming in the Canadian forests as applicable to similar farming in the United States.

PURCHASE OF LAND

The English government has appointed so-called "crown land agents" for various districts to point out and sell public land. In all towns you can get information on where they are to be found. The price per acre may vary from 20 cents to $1.00, depending on quality and location. One-fifth of the purchase sum is paid in cash and the rest in five years with interest. There is the added condition that the buyer live at least two years on the land, cultivate ten acres and build a house at least sixteen-by-twenty feet fit for human habitation. If these conditions are not fulfilled, the land may revert to the government. The government will also give away land free of charge, so-called "free grants." The conditions are that you must be at least eighteen; the land must be taken within a month after the grant; twelve acres must be cultivated within four years; a log cabin sixteen by twenty feet must be built on the land; and you must live there until these conditions have been fulfilled. The districts I visited that offered such free grants were remote from other settlements and the soil was third class. Therefore I cannot recommend these free grants to my countrymen. I have referred to company or speculator land above, the price varies from $4.00 to $10 an acre.

ACROSS THE PENINSULA TO THE
WESTERN BORDER OF CANADA

On August 9 we again continued our excursion, now returning south after having visited many settlers and made a tour of the districts towards the north and the west where all trees still die of natural causes. However, the time will soon come when the land all the way to Parry Sound and the Magnetawan River will have been settled. On our return south we entered a canoe at the Severn River in order to get to Sparrow Lake a few miles away. Along the shores of this lake and in its shallow waters, which gradually blended with miles and miles of swamp land, there grows a grass with an edible kernel. This grain is called water rice and is very popular with the Indians. When the grass is ripe the Indians glide through the grass in their canoes, bend the tops over the gunwale, and rub or knock the kernels into the boat. Seed-eating birds also flock in great numbers to such watery fields where they are hunted and killed with ease.

The general state of health seemed to be good even though I did come across some settlers with malaria. More often we met people who were temporary invalids because of axe cuts in legs or arms. Inexperience or reckless handling of these long and heavy axes was as much to blame for this as unpredictable accidents. Emigrants from Scotland and Ireland were dominant, but there were some scattered settlements of Germans. No settlement was more than a few years old. The town lots at the Muskoka Falls were surveyed while I was there. Obviously the settlers still had many difficulties to struggle with, for the law ceases where the forest begins. There is no authority to enforce the laws that have been made many hundreds of miles away. The few roads built by the government were very poor. The settlers themselves are responsible for the upkeep of roads two years after they have been built, but this is neglected to such a degree that people came all the way from the inland districts near Lake Huron to settle along lakes or rivers where they could have water transportation. Had you, dear reader, spent a day driving over cordwood roads where no log was less than eighteen inches in diameter and where the surface had not been planed – had you in other words driven an entire day on miles and miles of logs – then you would not be in any need of a recipe for the tenderizing of human flesh.

As I now take farewell of life in the woods I still have a few words of advice for my countrymen who have time and money to spend among pioneers in the forest. Should you be camping out of doors the fire in front of your bark lean-to will be your friend for the night. Do not let it die; otherwise the dragoons of the air, the mosquitoes, and their infantry, the invisible sand flies, will ravage and devastate that battlefield on your body otherwise known as your face. Your dreams will be uneasy and frightening, depending on how near your ears are the trumpet blasts of the mosquitoes. Should you seek rest in a backwoods tavern, you should be prepared for the draughts of an open attic. From the downstairs saloon you will climb up a ladder to the attic where you will see double beds in a row, a view that reminds the bachelor of his lack of a life companion and the married man of his absent wife. If there are no panes in the windows or perhaps not even frames, you should confer with your health about how much draught you may survive. Should you, too, have to make do with this American luxury, you might try hanging your shirt over the window, for the hotel will certainly not have anything to offer. When you get up in the morning you should make a thorough search of your clothes, not so much to find out if anything has been lost but to see if you have acquired anything – and I am referring to vermin. Like the potato, the bedbug seems to have its home in America. They are to be found everywhere, in towns as well as in the countryside. If you shake a juniper they will emerge from the earth in their green uniforms and if you take a look beneath the sheets of a bed they will assemble in their well-known coffee-brown dress. Even Quebec does not seem to have the water necessary to get rid of them and what could one then expect of the rest of the country that cannot draw upon the St Lawrence!

Early in the morning, at five o'clock, a bell, gong-gong, or another nerve-racking instrument is sounded to wake you up. Half an hour later there is more noise and this is the signal for breakfast. Never delay rising from your bed, for should you be late for breakfast the best pieces of pork and beaf will have disappeared. Indeed, you may even run the risk of entirely missing your morning dinner, as the first solid meal for the day may be called with some accuracy. Far from civilization, only pork will be served, however, and for every meal at that, along with cold or hot wheat bread, coffee, or tea. To begin with, I reacted against all the meat since I am not used to such an abundance; but now I have developed from being an eater of bread to becoming a meat-eater and I will frequently enjoy a steak without any bread for breakfast. For dinner the meat courses are often followed by a variety of pies or puddings but never by soup. In summer iced water takes the place of soup. The evening meal does not offer any variety in the dishes served. Apple or berry conserves may then be served with cold meat. No meal is enjoyed at leisure. There is a story about a man who took the biblical curse of eating your bread in the sweat of your brow literally and never sat down to a meal before he had worked himself into a sweat – even in coldest winter. The American, however, gets even closer to Scripture since he seems to regard the meal itself as labour. He does not taste his food, enjoy it, or season it with pleasant conversation. He quite simply gobbles it down and leaves the gluttony – the dining-room – without ceremony as soon as he is finished.

The servants are without experience, nor do they behave as servants. Families are consequently getting new maids all the time. Haughty, lazy, and ignorant, these girls nevertheless have requirements that any civilized housewife must deny them. A lady in Toronto once told me that one day she asked the maid to lay the table for ten people as they were expecting guests for dinner. On inspecting the table she found places for eleven. She assumed that the maid had made a mistake and asked her to correct it, but the maid refused and it was discovered that she had laid the eleventh place for herself – a manœuvre, however, that was not successful in this family. Consequently, many families prefer to manage without servants. An important reason for the pretenses as well as the carelessness of servants is that many a mistress has herself often started out in this country in the same position and that the servants therefore regard her as their equal. Families from Europe who are used to the comforts provided by good servants will have to relinquish this convenience in America, and poor emigrants who take work as servants in order to make a living on arrival will discover that this work is incomparably more comfortable, easier, and more profitable than in the old country.

On several occasions I had met with Mr Fleming, an engineer in Toronto.[18] He had been in England that summer with the plans for a railroad from the Selkirk settlements just north of the border to Minnesota and east to Lake Superior. He had led me to expect that I would be allowed to accompany him to these distant parts, more specifically to the valley of the Saskatchewan River. There is strong interest in Canada to enter a close union with these vast regions. In order to expedite my membership in this expedition he recommended that I accompany him to Montreal, where we were to meet the head of the expedition. But my hopes were dashed since the head of the expedition had been called to England and had left a telegram ordering Mr Fleming to come to London as soon as possible. The expedition was going to be delayed for an unspecified length of time, so I left Montreal that same evening and continued without further delay through Toronto and westward to the town of Guelph, about forty-five miles away. My sole profit from this journey of seven hundred miles was confirmation of the old adage that to and fro are of equal length.

My only remaining task is to describe the western section of the peninsula of Western Canada, from Lake Erie in the south to Lake Huron in the north. From an agronomic point of view this is at present the most important part of all of Canada. The soil is mostly a mixture of clay and mould. Hardwood forests still cover most of the peninsula, but on many of the established farms you may see fields and meadows without stumps. As in other parts of Canada, however, the newcomer will have to clear virgin forest. Almost all land had been bought by speculators or private land companies who were now selling forest land at from $8.00 to $18 an acre. Germans, Dutchmen, and British have had the insight to settle on the peninsula, apparently, with capital. Among the flourishing settlements I may mention Guelph, Breslau, Berlin, Peterborough,[19] Baden, and Hamburg, names that remind us of the strong German element in the population. Even though the peninsula stands at the head of the annual statistics as the yolk of Canada, these promising figures hold no promise for the Scandinavian emigrant without cash capital. Not many can afford to buy land and get through the first difficult years, and the thirty bushels of wheat per acre that the virgin forest soil will yield can be had at less expense and less effort from cheaper and more convenient land. I have made several excursions on the peninsula, but my impression of it as a home for the emigrant was everywhere the same.

In the middle of August I finally stood at the border of the United States. Before I said goodbye to Canada I added some beautiful pebbles from the river bank at Port Sarnia to my collection of rocks. On the rapid currents of the river I observed steamships from Chicago and other towns by the Great Lakes, and all the sailing ships that passed through the sound provided entertainment for the eye. Most sailing ships made use of tugboats going upriver; few attempted to sneak along the shores up to the mouth of Lake Huron with the wind as their only source of locomotion. I was told that the Norwegian clipper *Sleipner* out of Bergen has never yet made use of steam assistance to force its way up the strong current.[20]

This is not the place to decide whether or not the emigrant should settle in Canada, for the country of comparison, the United States, has yet to be described. But in comparison with Norway, Sweden, and Denmark, Canada must in my view take an unqualified first place. In none of these old countries can the man without means acquire land of such good quality under such cheap conditions, and the ability of Canadian soil to yield wheat year after year without being fertilized is convincing evidence that this country is far more fertile than Scandinavia. Canada has a liberal system of government and the authorities have the power to protect the land and its citizens. Since it is in the interest of Canada to promote settlement of the country, the government is more responsive to the reasonable demands of its settlers than is the case in the neighbouring United States.

Notes

PART 1 INTRODUCTION

1. The Canadian Discovery of Norway

1 Gates (1934) is still the best survey of government involvement in immigration promotion before Confederation. On Rolph, see Cowan (1961, 123-7). For the promotion of immigration from Scandinavia after Confederation, see Jalava (1983) and Ljungmark (1982).

2 Fischer and Nordvik (1985) and Knaplund (1931); Holand (1930, 20-6) gives an anecdotal account of several Norwegians in North American from the seventeenth century, including Willard Ferdinand Wentzel, agent for the North-West Company and member of several expeditions in the North-West, and the establishing of Norway House on the Nelson River. Stafford and Naess (1984, 20-31) have translated the memoirs of a Norwegian sailor who jumped ship in Quebec in 1846 and spent about a year wandering around and finding various employment in Canada before entering the United States.

3 All quotations from official Canadian documents refer to the Appendixes of the *Journals of the Legislative Assembly of the Province of Canada* and, after 1860, to the *Sessional Papers of the Parliament of the Province of Canada*. These appendixes and papers are as a rule unpaginated, but each volume has an alphabetical index as well as a list of contents. No further references will be made to these documents when cited. The annual reports are in the volumes for the following year. From 1862 on, Buchanan's report is included in the report from the Minister of Agriculture.

4 In his report for 1858 Closter made the same point in his somewhat tortured syntax: "The causes of adopting this Port, as a more favourable one than New York, are owing to the readiness of obtaining cargo, on return home, as well as the facility offered by the St Lawrence, to forwad the passengers westwards."

5 The four other ports were Hamburg, Liverpool, an Irish port, and New York. The third of these committees was an attempt to pacify French Canadian opposition to the one-sided Anglophone or Protestant addresses of most immigration promotion schemes, and it recommended the appointment of agents in France, Belgium, and Switzerland. The agent eventually sent to France, however, was unable to function because of the obstructions raised by the French authorities.

Christiania, after 1877 spelled Kristiania, was renamed Oslo in 1925.

2. Early Norwegian Settlements in Canada

1 The following account of the settlements in the Eastern Townships and Gaspé is indebted to Blegen's research.

2 Tambs had lived for several years in England before he immigrated again to Canada with his English wife and their four children in 1852. He eventually settled in Ontario, where he died in 1872 (Wicklund 1967).

3 There is no mention of Norwegians going to the Eastern Settlements in Buchanan's reports for 1855 or 1856, while the "young men" are accounted for in his report for 1857. The information about the 1857 group that Tambs brought is in the Norwegian subagent's report for 1858, included in the report from Buchanan. Norlie (1925, 252) names the leader of the Norwegians settling in Bury in 1857 as a Captain John Svendsen. Johan Schrøder, who spent some days in the company of Tambs and his family when he visited Bury in the Eastern Townships, tells of a group of Norwegians who settled there in 1856, but this reference, repeated by several historians, is probably to the 1857 group.

4 Closter had apparently been offered employment in 1856 but had been busy with his own affairs. See report on a lecture Closter gave in Stavanger, Norway, in *Morgenbladet* 2 May 1861.

5 The spelling of place names has been corrected. Telemark is south-east of Oslo; Lofoten, the base for rich cod fisheries, is a string of islands jutting out from the northern coast; and Vardø is in the extreme northeast, not far from the Russian border. Probably Haugan concentrated his efforts on Trondheim and the surrounding area because a good number of the Norwegians who had settled in the Eastern Townships were from Selbu, a parish north of Trondheim, and because a couple of fishermen from that area had been persuaded to settle in Gaspé the year before (Dietrichson 1861; Norlie 1925, 252–3).

6 The fact that the money they had received for necessary provisions was given in return for notes "payable in labor" may have been one reason some chose to leave as soon as possible. (See the chapter on "Proposed Works" in the report from the Commissioner of Crown Lands for 1861.)

7 Such items were repeated in other newspapers; these three also appeared in such Christiania papers as *Morgenbladet* and *Aftenposten*.

8 The fisheries in Gaspé, however, were very different from the small-scale fisheries on the Norwegian coast, where ownership was local, the fishermen often being part owners themselves. In Gaspé a few large firms had a virtual monopoly on the fisheries as well as on the marketing of all fish at home and abroad. These large companies "could keep out small competitors and control both the price of fish and the economic life of their employees" (Innes 1954, 179).

9 For instance *Stavanger Amtstidende og Adresseavis* 31 December 1860 and *Menneskevennen* 1 (January 1861).

10 In Stavanger several papers brought reports and the most complete one, in *Stavangeren*, was reprinted by *Morgenbladet* (2 May 1861) in the capital.

11 Gaspé County had no so-called "colonization roads" before 1858. The roads serving the area settled by the Norwegians were begun the summer of 1860 but were scarcely roads in any current sense of the word. In the report from the Minister of Agriculture for 1862 they are characterized as "paths into the interior of the forest for emigrants having no other means of transport but their backs to carry all their effects."

12 In the report of the Commissioner of Crown Lands for 1861 the account of "The Norwegians' Roads" estimates that "during the present year about 400 settlers, from Norway and Sweden, and a few from New Brunswick" had come to the area.

13 Eden's report is quoted by Buchanan, whose report for 1862 forms part of the report from the Minister of Agriculture.

14 Letters from Asbjørn Kloster to his parents, his brother, and Charles Shieldstream in Gaspé are in the Oslo University Library. Blegen makes use of correspondence to Kloster in the Quaker Archives in Stavanger. Kloster provided for the return passage of his parents late in the summer of 1862.

15 Some information on Jacobson's visit to Quebec and to Gaspé in 1862 may be found in the Abraham Jacobson Papers, Norwegian–American Historical Association. In addition to several letters, there is an essay by his daughter, Clara Jacobson, "Fra svundne Dage" (1929).

3. Canada in Norway

1 For instance: "Early morning 4 June we came to the Newfoundland banks where we had calm weather and where we spent the whole day fishing a large quantity of cod, about 500 fishes, so that all onboard had more than enough fish to eat. I had the captain's fishing gear for a short while and hauled 8 large fishes" (NHKI MS, 6 August 1855).

2 For instance *Almuevennen* 11 (1859): 377–8, which presents an engraving entitled "A Picture from Canada in North America" with a settler's log cabin right next to an Indian wigwam by a river and with Indians and white settlers, both equally exotic, gathered behind a canoe in the foreground.

Norwegian readers would not have made any connection between the strange life depicted here and the life in North America with which they were familiar through letters. As a sidelight on the fictitious nature of such features and on the uninhibited borrowing of material in the press, it may be mentioned that this engraving is obviously based on the engraving by W.H. Bartlett that is used as the frontispiece of his *Canadian Scenery Illustrated* (1842). In the original, however, the "log cabin" appears as one of several wigwams and only Indians are depicted.

3 *Prairie Farming in America*, published in London in 1859, was based on travels in Canada and the United States. Caird's title seems to have obscured the fact that his book is essentially a travel account, and it is not included in the bibliography of books by visitors to the Canadian provinces in Gerald Craig's *Early Travellers in the Canadas, 1791–1867*. A Danish edition was published the same year in Copenhagen, the main publishing center for Norway as well as Denmark throughout the nineteenth century. A collation suggests that Schrøder used this translated text with some amendments for his journal.

4. Johan Schrøder and His Book

1 The preliminary one-year course (*examen philosophicum*) was required before acceptance to the more specialized degree courses in medicine, theology, philology, natural sciences, or law. The preliminary examinations included questions in philosophy, mathematics, astronomy, physics, chemistry, and natural history. Some biographical information is from the scant sketches of both Schrøder and his father in Halvorsen (1901).

2 In turning to letters he was following in the footsteps of his father, who had translated Goethe, published on political and legal issues, and edited a dictionary of all personnel in the armed forces.

3 For instance in the *Quebec Gazette* for 20 June and the Montreal *Gazette* for 26 June.

4 See Part 2, Introduction, for a translation of the introduction that Schrøder wrote for this series.

5 This notice also specified from which settlements information already had been received. A similar notice appeared in the first issue of the Chicago newspaper *Marcus Thrane's Norske Amerikaner* 25 May 1866.

6 By this time book distribution and publishing in Norwegian was fairly well established among the immigrants in the midwestern United States. For an account of the early history of this publishing, including the role of Schrøder, see Øverland (1986).

7 See *Emigranten* 25 December 1865 and 8 January 1866. Monsen actually published his *Calendar of Names*, containing addresses as well as entertaining reading, at the end of the year. See 15 November 1866.

8 A copy of the publisher's circular advertising Schrøder's book and inviting subscriptions is in the University Library, Oslo. The Swedish edition, published in Stockholm in 1868, is an abbreviated translation.

9 Norwegian immigrants in North America seem to have adapted quite comfortably to the prevalent anti-Irish prejudices. The first history of the Norwegian migrations and settlements in the United States, published as a series of instalments in the illustrated journal *Billed–Magazin* (Madison, Wis. 1868–70) by the editor, Svein Nilsson, not only is in the filio-pietistic mode so common in early immigrant histories but revels in derogatory comments on "the sons of Erin." The Norwegian–American novelist Ole Edvart Rølvaag's trilogy, beginning with *Giants in the Earth* (English translation 1927), suffers from implicit prejudice against the Irish, while in a novel by H.A. Foss, *Valborg* (Decorah, Iowa 1927, no English translation), the second generation's defection from the ways of their immigrant parents is indicated by their inclination to enjoy ragtime and marry Irishmen.

10 In fact, the soils of southern Ontario "tended to be far better than those of the St. Lawrence lowland, but were not really as rich as the long-grass prairie soils of parts of the American Middle West" (Harris 1974, 115–16).

11 Some years before Schrøder travelled in Canada, in 1839–42, a young Norwegian theologian and natural scientist, Peter M. Stuwitz, had been in Newfoundland, St Pierre, and Labrador as head of a two-man delegation appointed by the Norwegian government to study the organization of the Newfoundland fisheries. After having extended his stay in North America beyond the one year stipulated by his employers, Stuwitz became ill and died in Newfoundland. His reports and papers are in the Norwegian National Archives and Bergen University Library, and a complete edition of Peter M. Stuwitz's reports, diaries, and correspondence from Newfoundland is being prepared by Lewis R. Fischer of Memorial University and Helge W. Nordvik of the University of Bergen. The two have published an initial presentation of Stuwitz and his work in Newfoundland (Fischer and Nordvik 1985b).

PART 2 JOHAN SCHRØDER

Introduction to a "Book for Scandinavians at Home and in America" in Emigranten *1863*

1 The first version of Schrøder's book was printed in three instalments in *Emigranten* 5–19 October 1863 as "En Bog for Nordboerne hjemme og i Amerika" ("A Book for Scandinavians at Home and in America"). The planned title for the complete work, expected to be published later in the same year, is "Dagbog i Amerika" ("American Diary"). The introduction

seems to have been written by Schrøder even though he is referred to in the third person. The extract given here is from the concluding two columns in which Schrøder explains his intentions. The preceding columns present a brief account of the reasons for emigration and the debate on emigration in Norway.

Schrøder consistently used the terms "emigrant" and "emigration," here as well as in his book. This was also the usage of most contemporary Norwegian immigrants in North America who tended define themselves as having left their former country rather than as having entered their new one.

1. Across the Atlantic

1 According to Norwegian and Icelandic tradition Ganger Rolf was the name of the Norwegian Viking chieftan, Rollo (Old Norse: Hrolfr), who founded the Norman duchy in France in 911. The owners of *Ganger Rolf*, Det Søndenfjelds–Norske Dampskibsselskab, were pioneers in the very modest beginnings of Norwegian international steamship lines, and this ship had served the Christiania–Hull route since 1856. When Schrøder began his journey there was a weekly service on this route in co-operation with a Hull company, Thos. Wilson Sons & Co., owners of the *Scandinavian* and the main feeders of the steerage quarters of the liners departing from Liverpool for Quebec with passengers from Continental Europe via Hull and rail (Gibbs 1963, 540). Newspaper advertisements reveal that the Christiania agent for the Hull service, A. Sharpe & Co, was agent for the Allan Line (Montreal Ocean Steam Ship Company) as well as for the British American Land Company.

  Schrøder had visited England the previous year by the same route. See Part 2, Introduction.
2 Christiansand, now Kristiansand, is a town near the southern tip of Norway.
3 The departure from Liverpool was 11 June (Montreal *Gazette* 20 June 1863). According to the same news notice, the stop in Ireland was at Queenstown, in the south, not Londonderry, in the north, as Schrøder has it. The *Bohemian*, built in 1859, belonged to the Montreal Ocean Steam Ship Company, later, the Allan Line. It was lost near Cape Elizabeth on 22 February 1864. The Allan Line had weekly sailings Liverpool–Montreal, but immigrants during this period disembarked at Quebec (Gibbs 1963, 284–7).
4 By regulation all steerage passengers were forbidden to take alcoholic beverages on board ship.
5 The transportation of destitute or delinquent children from the United Kingdom to the colonies on a regular basis had begun in the 1830s. One institution that shipped boys to Quebec was the London Ragged School.

In the two years preceding Schrøder's voyage the annual number of reformatory school boys arriving in Quebec was sixty-five (Cowan 1961, 221-3).

6 The italicized words are in English in Schrøder's text.

7 The *Anglo Saxon*, built 1856, foundered near Cape Henry on 27 April 1963. Of the four hundred and forty-five persons on board, two hundred and thirty-eight were lost (Gibbs 1963, 287). The wreck of the *Anglo Saxon*, its possible causes, and the question of responsibility were still being discussed in Canadian newspapers when Schrøder arrived.

8 The *Bohemian* was met by the news yacht of the Associated Press at Cape Race, south-east of the Avalon Peninsula, Newfoundland, on 19 June (Montreal *Gazette*, 20 June 1863). The telegraph cables that brought the news into Canada had been laid in 1856.

9 The *Norwegian*, built in 1861, was wrecked on St Paul Island, Cabot Strait, 14 June 1863 (Gibbs 1963, 287).

10 As a steerage passenger Schrøder obviously did not have direct access to information about what was going on. It is correct that the *Bohemian* received news about the wreck at Cape Race, but meanwhile the *St Andrew*, which belonged to the same line, had seen flares from the *Norwegian* and gone to help. It had already taken on board two hundred passengers, leaving a hundred and four passengers and forty members of the crew to the *Bohemian*. The captain remained at the wreck with some of his crew. There was a controversy in the papers concerning the behaviour of the crew after the wreck. While a group of steerage passengers published a statement highly critical of the captain for his neglect in taking care of the passengers' property and keeping discipline among his crew, this was countered with a letter signed by first-class passengers praising the ship's officers. The irresponsible behaviour of the crew would seem to have been a response to the policy of the shipowners, whose contractual responsibility was annulled in case of a wreck. On 9 July the Montreal *Gazette* could report that the four engineers and twenty-one firemen who were the last to leave the wreck of the *Norwegian* had been brought into Halifax by a naval vessel. They sent a telegram to the owners in Montreal who wired back that they had no further use for their services and no responsibility for them. Eventually the twenty-five crew members were sent back to England at the expense of William Cunard. By this time ads for the Montreal Ocean Steam Ship Company had ceased to appear in the *Gazette*.

11 For Schrøder's account of the failed Norwegian settlement at Gaspé, see Part 2, Chapter 4. For a brief history of this settlement, see Part 1, Chapter 2.

12 Although the great majority of Norwegian immigrants were still crossing the Atlantic on sailing ships, in 1863 the proportion of all immigrants "who crossed to Canada in steamships was forty-six per cent., in 1869 it was ninety-five per cent., and in 1875 all immigrants came by steamship" (Innis

1954, 203). Schrøder's advice seems to have been based on the radical change in choice of conveyance, also by Norwegians, obvious at the time he completed his book in 1867.

13 The *speciedaler* was a Norwegian silver coin in use until 1873, when its value was set to four *kroner*. It was the equivalent of 0.224 pounds sterling.

2. Canada East or Lower Canada

1 The Grand Trunk Railway Company was incorporated in 1852–3 and became the main railway system of the Province of Canada. At the time of Schrøder's journey it had lines from Sarnia in the west to Portland, Maine, in the east, but was in financial difficulties.

2 An instance of material added to the book while Schrøder was completing his book in Wisconsin. Bergen, the second largest city in Norway, is on the west coast; Østerdal, a long valley, is in the southeast.

3 Schrøder gave such information in the United States section of his book, which is not included in this edition.

4 Schrøder's historical survey is not only brief but inaccurate. Thus he gave 1534 as the year for Cartier's first voyage, had Kirk [*sic*] taking Quebec in 1729, and gave 1761 as the year for the Peace of Paris. Such errors have been corrected in this edition.

5 The area covered by Lower and Upper Canada was smaller than that of the two provinces of Quebec and Ontario today. The area of Norway is 323,895 Km^2. Schrøder confuses Upper and Lower Canada here and this has been corrected.

6 "By 1860 intoxicants had been banished from the lumber camp list of rations almost everywhere and the camps were models of sobriety. The shantyman and raftsman had to control their impatience as best they might until they got down to civilization again. Then ... they were able to resume their liberties." Lower (1973, 185–96) gives an account of the life and lore of the raftsmen of this period. The quotation is from p. 193.

7 The rhyme is in English in the original.

8 Western Abnaki still live at Odanak on the St-François River where Schrøder visited their village in 1863.

9 The hunting lands of the Western Abnaki had since 1830 been in the area of the L'Assomption, Maskinongé, Maurice, and Vermillion rivers on the north side of the St Lawrence.

10 Peter Paul Osunkhirhine (or Pial Wzôkhilain, as his name is also transliterated) was hardly a shaman in the sense in which this word is generally used. On the contrary, he worked as a Protestant missionary and teacher among the Western Abnaki after he had attended Moore's Charity School in Hanover, New Hamsphire. In the period 1830–44 Osunkhirhine translated and published several books, mainly religious, into the Penobscot

dialect of the Abnaki. Osunkhirhine is given brief mention in Trigger (1978, 152) and a separate entry in Hodge (1910). L'Abbé J.A. Maurault gives a long polemical account of Osunkhirhine's work as Protestant missionary in his 1866 *Histoire des Abénakis*. That Schrøder should be so impressed by this elderly gentleman speaks of his open mind; that he should remain so ignorant of Osunkhirhine's true position among his people is suggestive of Schrøder's limited understanding of what he saw.

11 The Abnaki village at Odanak is "not older than 1660" (Trigger 1978, 153).

12 Illness of a malarial character. Schrøder added the English "ague and fever" in parentheses.

13 "In the War of 1812, the Abnakis of St. Francis and Bécancour furnished two companies for the British forces, and they now refer to their participation as 'the last time the Abenakis went to war' ..." (Trigger 1978, 152).

14 According to the most recent official statistics, there had been two hundred and seventy-one inhabitants in the village in 1861, down from three hundred and eighty-seven in 1858.

15 Schrøder's implicit comparison was with the far lighter summer nights of Norway.

16 Schrøder had this idiom in English and added the Norwegian word for top hat in parentheses.

17 Schrøder was following an established literary convention of rendering descriptions of an indelicate nature in Latin in order not to offend the uneducated reader. The Indians were, in plain English, stark naked.

18 The italicized words spoken by the young Indians are in Schrøder's English.

19 While the Civil War had little effect on Norwegian immigration to the United States, news of the Sioux uprising in 1862 led to a temporary decline in 1863, the year of the Homestead Act. Letters from panic-stricken Minnesota immigrants were published in Norwegian newspapers in the fall and winter before Schrøder began his voyage.

20 On this scale 0 degrees is the freezing point and 80 degrees the boiling point for water.

21 Alexander Carlisle Buchanan. See Part 1, Chapters 1 and 2.

22 Charles John Brydges (1827–89) came to Canada as general manager of the Great Western Railway in 1852 and was general manager of the Grand Trunk Railway, 1862–79.

23 Gjertsen was captain on the brig *Haabet*, which had arrived in ballast from Halifax on 15 June, according to the *Montreal Herald* for the following day. Its departure with wheat and deals was noted by the same newspaper on 7 July. Tromsø is a town on an island in the far north of Norway.

24 Helge Haugan. See Part 1, Chapters 1 and 2.

25 Complaints against emigration agents and runners were frequently published in Norwegian and Norwegian–American newspapers by dissatisfied emigrants. See Part 1, Chapter 2.

3. Lower Canada South of the St Lawrence River

1 The Victoria Railway Bridge at Montreal was built by the Grand Trunk and opened to regular traffic in 1859.

2 Schrøder was, of course, being facetious. Although the seigneurial system had been formally abolished ten years earlier, there had been little real change since most tenants could not afford to pay the seigneur the value of their land and continued to pay rent (Harris and Warkentin 1974, 68).

3 See Part 1, Chapter 2, on the Norwegian settlement in the Eastern Townships. Schrøder's evaluation of the relative quality of the soil reflects accepted opinion (Harris and Warkentin 1974, 96).

4 A town in south-eastern Norway, close to the Swedish border. The present name of the town is Halden.

5 The British American Land Company had acquired its original grant of crown land in the Eastern Townships in 1834. Although they were forced to relinquish a large part of their original grant in 1841, they still controlled a significant section of the Townships through subsequent purchases. Sherbrooke had been the site of the Company's Canadian headquarters since 1837.

6 Such metereological observations speak of nostalgia rather than insight. Moreover, the direction of breezes from the mountains would of course depend on where you were situated in relation to the mountains. Schrøder's point of view would be the southern and south-eastern parts of Norway.

7 Schrøder's views below are much the same as those found in Day's *History of the Eastern Townships*, written only a few years later. In her account of the mineral resources she, too, commented on the preoccupation with "what is but imaginative and speculative" (1869, 245) and in telling how "wild and fanatical theories have at times been introduced" by Protestant preachers, she observed that "perhaps some of them are entitled to the credit of having believed in the truth and consistency of theories they advanced and urged upon others; but the event has proved, that not all thus employed have been deserving of even this consideration."

8 Schrøder did not specify any monetary unit.

9 Not identified. In 1867 the Norwegian agents of the British American Land Company refer to statements by a company agent named A.W. Henecke in a polemic on the quality of the land in the Eastern Townships (*Morgenbladet* 21 February). Either or both could be misspellings of the same name.

10 Farsund is a small coastal town in southern Norway. Schrøder's spelling of "Eiken" is "Egen" and he specifies the distance as five miles from Farsund. The name Andersdatter means the daughter of Anders.

11 Cornelius Helgenius Tambs. See Part 1, Chapter 2. Joseph Pennoyer was a Provincial Surveyor, also in the employ of the British American Land

Company. Several of his maps and town plans are listed by O'Bready (1973). William Farwell had been appointed Crown Land Agent in Compton in September 1861. His status as such was exceptional in that the Commissioner's report for 1863 shows that he received a salary of $600, while most other agents worked on a commission basis, a few also receiving a modest per diem.

12 See Russell (1973) pp. 179–82 for an account of Canadian stage-coaches.

13 Not quite accurate. See Part 1, Chapter 2, note 3.

14 Christopher Closter. See Part 1, Chapter 2.

15 Schrøder met Zimmermann later in Portland and was not impressed with his knowledge of agriculture.

16 A small town on the southern coast of Norway.

17 In Norway, however, farmers with small holdings collected twigs with leaves that were dried and bundled for use as winter fodder far into this century.

18 Here Schrøder was voicing current opinion in the Eastern Townships. Thus Mrs Day (1869, 239), wrote of the desirability to get settlers "to take these partially improved [abandoned] farms and cultivate them with skill and energy. Such lands can always be had, and are usually worth the money asked for them." The editor of the *Sherbrooke Gazette* saw the purchase of lots "where some considerable improvements have been made" as a way to solve the problems of both parties to the transaction: The original settler, impoverished but with experience in clearing land, could get sufficient capital to pay outright for new land and start all over again, while the newcomer "is not thrown into circumstances where his previous knowledge and experience is useless to him" (29 August 1863).

19 A county north of present-day Oslo.

20 Schrøder was alluding here to his own recent experience. See Part 1, Chapter 4.

21 John Henry Pope (1819–89) was a native of Eaton Township and represented Compton, first in the Legislative Assembly and then in the House of Commons, from 1857 to his death. He served twice (1871–3 and 1878–85) as Minister of Agriculture and his interest in this aspect of government is reflected in his conversation with Schrøder. When he met Schrøder he had just been returned by acclamation from Compton.

22 Lake Moffat is in the Township of Lingwick, which was still largely unsettled, with a mere five hundred and sixty-four inhabitants in 1861. The land was owned by the British American Land Company (Day 1869, 405–7).

23 Schrøder often remarked on the neglect to fertilize fields in Canada, as did many other contemporary commentators. Russell observes that while fertilizer was not necessary for the first two or three years after clearing, "most farmers still neglected this important aid to good harvest" in the following years. "In French Canada the authorities railed against the habi-

tants who would not use the abundant manure provided by their cattle ...
Visitors to English Canada noted huge piles of accumulated manure that
eventually forced the farmer to move his barn" (1973, 36–7).

24 East of Oslo.

25 See Part 1, Chapter 2, for an account of emigration agents in Quebec.

26 The main agent, A.C. Buchanan, was appointed by and answered to the
    Canadian government. See Part 1, Chapter 1.

27 This duty was an effect of the British Poor Act amendments of 1834 "which
    permitted the removal of workhouse inmates" and which encouraged the
    Poor Law unions to send destitute women to the colonies. On occasion
    Buchanan would protest that many of those sent were unemployable.
    (Cowan 1961, 223–4; also Johnson [1913], 255–7).

28 That spring a shed for single women had been added to the new immi-
    grant facilities at the Old Custom House. See Part 1, Chapter 2.

4. From Quebec Eastward to the Sea

1 The original has "south-east," but this is clearly an error.

2 See Part 1, Chapter 2.

3 The italicized phrase is identical with the original.

4 There was no steamship landing at Cacouna and all traffic to this popular
   resort went by way of Rivière-du-Loup.

5 In "Notes of a Trip to Cacouna" in the Montreal *Gazette* (13 August 1863)
   the journalist observes: "There is an Indian encampment off the beach.
   They are busy making baskets, beads and trinkets for the visitors. They
   are fine looking people; quiet, civil and sober, but very ignorant and in
   great poverty – all Roman Catholics, and can neither read nor write – have
   no schools, and the poor children are growing up as their ancestors in
   barbarism, idleness and ignorance." Although Schrøder does not appear
   to have shared the journalist's racial prejudices, he did share his
   anti-Catholicism.

6 Carried away by his speculations on the imagined promiscuity of these
   Indian women, Schrøder here used a lame and untranslatable pun on the
   Norwegian idiom "to give a man the basket," meaning to refuse a suitor.
   He meant simply that these women *sold* their baskets.

7 The Maliseets (or Malecites), who cultivated corn at the time of the
   European conquest of their land, now live in northern New Brunswick
   and Quebec.

8 This was no doubt the red seaweed dulse, still dried and eaten raw as a
   snack or delicacy along the North Atlantic coast. Dulse can also be prepared
   in a variety of ways as part of a meal. Due to impatience, Schrøder may
   have missed the full flavour of dulse, which becomes pronounced with
   prolonged chewing.

5. Up the Saguenay River to Lake St-Jean

1   "The magnificent iron steamer" *Magnet* began its season this year on 30 June and was advertising its "Grand excursion to the far-famed River Saguenay and sea-bathing at Murray Bay & Cacouna" in the newspapers of Montreal and Quebec at the time Schrøder was visiting these cities, for instance the Montreal *Gazette* 27 June. Stopping at Tadoussac, the *Magnet* returned from Ha! Ha! Bay. Tourist excursions on the Saguenay had been running regularly since 1849.

2   David Edward Price (1826–83) represented Chicoutimi and Saguenay, first in the Legislative Assembly, later in the Council, from 1855 to 1867, when he was called to the Senate. He was the son of William Price, known as the Father of the Saguenay, founder of the major lumber firm that became Price Brothers Company on his death in 1867. Lower, who has a sub-chapter on "The Price Family" in his *Great Britain's Woodyard*, writes that William Price "was the industrial pioneer of that region (which includes not only the Saguenay River but also Lac St. Jean) and was the first to realize its possibilities and develop them ... So successful was he that the whole region became a sort of fief, with his company in the position of feudal overlord" (1973, 149).

3   Schrøder often had his names slightly wrong. Here, for instance, he called the twin cliffs or peaks "Eternity and Fraternity."

4   Lutheranism was and is the official faith of Norway and the Lutheran Church is a state institution.

5   Schrøder used this English word and explained its meaning.

6   "the corduroy road, named somewhat ironically after the soft, corded fabric ... was made by laying logs, usually those obtained by the original clearing, transversely across the roadway. As no attempt was made to face the logs, and little effort to grade them by diameter, the resultant surface was a series of humps and hollows, over which the vehicles proceeded by jolts and pitches. Logs became displaced, rotted, or sank into the mud, creating holes into which wheels descended with a crash, immobilizing the vehicle or even causing an upset. Many travellers in Canada, during the first half of the nineteenth century, recorded their unhappy recollections and even dangers on the corduroy road" (Russell 1973, 170–1).

6. Forestry

1   Commenting on the claim made by the lumber industry that they "cleared the land in advance for farmers," Lower observed, "What the lumberman did in the way of clearing land was to cut out all the best timber and leave an impassable tangle of tops and limbs through which coppice growth soon shot up" (1973, 103). "The Select Committee appointed to enquire into

and report on the State of the Lumber Trade of Canada, in relation to the Settlement of the Country" had issued a preliminary report that spring and had considered the "supposed difficulties between the lumber merchants and the settlers" and concluded that since "a complete community of interest exists, there need be no difficulty in arranging a system to the mutual satisfaction of both parties" (*Journals* 1863, App. 8).

2   A *speciedaler* was the equivalent of 0.224 pounds sterling.

3   At this point Schrøder gave a translation of the main conditions for timber licenses as issued by the Department of Crown Lands.

4   This was hardly a Canadian tradition but a local one, reflecting the power and status of David Price in his electoral district.

7. *A Visit to Portland in the United States*

1   Andrew Russell (1804–88) was the son of a crown lands agent who came to Canada in 1822. He was a surveyor and engineer before he became an Assistant Commissioner of Crown Lands in 1857.

2   William McDougall (1822–1905) became Commissioner of Crown Lands in 1862, had been elected to the Legislative Assembly in 1858, and retained a Parliamentary seat for most of the period up to 1882. For an account of McDougall's work in Sweden in 1873–4 as official Canadian emigration agent, see Ljungmark (1982, 24–6) and Jalava (1983, 5).

3   Not identified. This may be an error or misunderstanding on Schrøder's part. The only Kierulf who was lieutenant colonel in 1867 was Otto Richard Kierulf, who later became Prime Minister. There is no record, however, of his making any visit to Canada or North America.

4   See Part 1, Chapter 2.

5   Schrøder's prejudices concerning American manners would have found approval with many Canadians. A.G. Gilbert, a journalist with the Montreal *Evening Telegraph*, took the train from Montreal to Portland the year Schrøder published his book, and remarked of the "American ladies" returning from a visit to Canada that they were "enjoying a chat in the manner peculiar to their great nation, by talking as loudly as they can, with a total disregard to the other passengers on the car truly delightful. And the manner in which they guess, and calculate, and reckon, and wonder, and criticise, is as amusing to the listener as it is characteristic of the greatest Republic on the face of the earth. With them everything seems to be on the same large scale, even to assurance, tone of voice, and bad manners." After crossing the border, where the passengers changed trains, "it was very evident that Canada had been left behind. While the train waited, youths with long white or yellow dusters, broad checked trousers, and vulgar patent leather boots, with a rowdy hat cocked to one side and cigar in mouth, lounged about the station and stared impertinently, and told

of another country, and other fashions besides those of Canada. The divid-
ing line was not broad but the distinction was great'' (1867, 4–6).

6 Johan Sebastian Cammermeyer Welhaven (1807–73), prominent Norwegian
   poet, was also professor of philosophy at the university in Christiania.
   Schrøder's reflections and attempt at irony would be based on his memory
   of one of the lectures he attended while studying for his preliminary degree.

7 The appellation would seem to be a fiction. Although there has been no
   Norwegian settlement in Maine, promotion in the 1860s led to a Swedish
   settlement in Aroostook County.

8 The italicized phrase is in English.

9 Entering at Quebec on 5 July, Captain Svanøe had arrived in Montreal on
   the ninth with his barque *Kong Carl*, loaded with herring, oil, and tar and
   carrying one cabin and a hundred and eleven steerage passengers. His ship
   was cleared for departure for London with wheat and flour on 11 August
   (Montreal *Gazette* 8, 9 July; 12 August).

8. Canada West or Upper Canada

1 Three lines had been built to transport lumber: Cobourg–Peterborough,
   Port Hope–Lindsay; Toronto–Collingwood.

2 Catharine Parr Traill (1802–99). The reference is to *The Backwoods of
   Canada: Being Letters from the Wife of an Emigrant Officer; Illustrative
   of the Domestic Economy of British America* (London, 1836. Several later
   editions; German and French translations in 1837 and 1843.) Among the
   pamphlets the Bureau of Agriculture had translated to Norwegian, German,
   and French for distribution in these countries was Traill's *The Female
   Emigrant's Guide, and Hints on Canadian Housekeeping* (1854) and this
   may well be the way in which Schrøder first made her acquaintance
   (Macdonald 1966, 74–5; Gates 1934, 26).

3 The italicized word are in the original.

4 An English company, first chaired by the author of *Sam Slick*, Thomas
   Chandler Haliburton, the Canadian Land and Emigration Company had
   just purchased ten townships in Haliburton and Victoria counties from
   the Department of Crown Lands. It was never a successful venture. The
   quality of the land was relatively poor, roads were undeveloped, and there
   were free grants available on crown lands in adjoining townships in
   Haliburton and in Muskoka.

5 Hardly a director, Mr. Roche, a native of Toronto, had been appointed
   agent for the company in December 1861 (Murray 1963, 277n).

6 Settlement in Orillia began some years before 1839, when the Ojibwa
   Indians who lived there has been resettled in Rama, the reservation across
   the lake that Schrøder visited. Orillia was incorporated as a village in 1867.
   The rapid expansion and development of this part of Upper Canada are

brought out in the German traveller J.G. Kohl's observation a few years earlier that Orillia was "the last and most northerly settlement of Canada in the direction from Toronto" (1861, 65–6). In 1863 Schrøder visited a German settlement north of Orillia.

7 Richard J. Oliver is listed as Free Grant Agent for Muskoka Road in the Crown Lands Commissioner's reports from 1859.

8 In using "America" and "American" to include Canada as well as the United States, Schrøder conformed with the usage of most Norwegian emigrants, as may be seen in the discussion of their correspondence in Part 1, Chapter 3.

9 In the report from the Bureau of Agriculture for 1856, "midge" is given as the most important insect causing the devastation of crops.

10 The Indians at Rama were one of the three remaining bands of a tribe that, "having originally migrated from Lake Superior, occupied as their hunting ground, the vast tract stretching from Collin's Inlet on the north-eastern shore of the Georgian Bay to the northern limits of the land claimed by the Mississaguas." They had gradually surrendered their land and the sixteen-hundred-acre reservation at Rama had been purchased "by themselves out of their annuity" in 1838. The 1858 report of the "Special Commission ... to Investigate Indian Affairs in Canada" said of Rama that "it affords one of the most striking and lamentable instances of the deterioration which has taken place in the condition of the Indians ... The log houses built for them about 13 or 14 years ago, being badly constructed, are all going to decay." The inhabitants of the village "are dragging through a life disgraceful to humanity" (Murray 1963, 119–20).

11 The Rev. R. Brooking of the Wesleyan Methodist Society is listed as missionary at Rama in the list of "Schools for Indians" in the report of the Commissioner of Crown Lands for 1863. The 1858 report quoted in Note 10 above, said that the school, which then was the responsibility of another missionary, "is not taught more than half the time," according to information given by the Indians.

12 In his report of a tour of inspection the same year that Schrøder travelled the road, included in the report of the Department of Crown Lands for 1863, James Bridgland claimed that in spite of the money spent on improvements, "I am bound in candor to declare that the road is very far from being throughout even a good *bush* road."

13 One difficulty in evaluating the role in Canadian history of ethnic groups from countries other than the United Kingdom is their invisibility in contemporary records as well as in standard historical accounts. While Schrøder saw Gravenhurst as a German settlement, Germans are not mentioned in the many records and documents collected by Murray (1963), in the survey of *Places in Ontario* by Nick Mika and Helma Mika (1981), or in Boyer's *Early Days in Muskoka* (1970).

14 Augustus John Alport is reported to have arrived from New Zealand the year before Schrøder's visit, having purchased his land, "sight unseen, from the Crown, prior to leaving from England ... It is said that he ... built a substantial house and since there was no road to the property, he had the materials and furnishings brought across the ice of Lake Muskoka from Gravenhurst." When Muskoka became a municipality in 1869, Alport, or Squire Alport as he was often called, was the first reeve (Boyer 1970, 25–6). His seven-hundred-acre farm, "probably the best in Muskoka," was advertised for sale in 1870, and the advertisement in the Orillia *Northern Light* described it as "delightfully situated on the Muskoka Lake and River ... with a water frontage of about five miles, and within its boundaries there is a small lake, of nearly 100 acres, which offers great attraction to parties fond of fishing and shooting" (Murray 1963, lxxxii, 255).

15 This would seem to be in Bracebridge, at the North Falls of the Muskoka River, which Oliver, in his report to the Crown Lands Commissioner for 1862, claimed was "destined to become a village. A new Tavern, Store, Lumber Mill and other buildings are now in the course of erection, and water power leased for a foundry, grist mill, and other machinery." Reporting to the Commissioner the following year on a visit here in 1863, however, Inspector of Roads and Surveys James W. Bridgland called the mill "a poor, miserable affair."

16 Schrøder's low opinion of the hotel at the North Falls was not shared by Inspector Bridgland from the Department of Crown Lands who noted in his report for 1864 that "Two decent houses of accommodation already exist – one at the South – the other at the North Falls."

17 In the popular Norwegian ballad "Oleana" (1853) the expectations of those who went to the violin virtuoso Ole Bull's failed colony in Pennsylvania are satirized. Here baked pigs run around and offer ham to the hungry, the salmon leap into the pot, and the calves make themselves into dishes for the settlers, who have nothing to do but enjoy the food and drink.

18 Sandford Fleming (1827–1915), who had become a civil engineer and acquired considerable experience in railroad construction after emigrating from Scotland in 1845, and who had published the pamphlet *A Railway to the Pacific through British Territory* (1858), had just been appointed by the Canadian government to survey a route for the intercontinental railway discussed by representatives from Canada, Nova Scotia, and New Brunswick in London. These plans failed to materialize, however, and Fleming did not survey the West until 1872, then as chief engineer of the Canadian Pacific Railway.

19 Schrøder's reasons, geographical as well as etymological, for including Peterborough in this list are obscure.

20 In September 1862 the sixty-three-foot barque *Sleipner* was the second European ship to go the direct route from Europe to Chicago. It carried

immigrants as well as freight (mainly salted herring) and its brief stops in Montreal were noticed in Canadian newspapers. *Sleipner* repeated this voyage every year until 1865. In 1863 its arrival at Montreal was noted in the Montreal *Gazette* on 15 June, a few days before Schrøder disembarked from the *Bohemian*. The second Norwegian ship to undertake this voyage, however, received even more attention than *Sleipner*. This was the fifty-one-register-ton sloop *Skjoldmøen*, also of Bergen. When the captain reported to customs in Quebec on 12 June 1863, he was at first not believed when he claimed to have come from Norway in such a small vessel. A third Bergen ship, the brig *Vidar*, made the voyage in 1866 as the last Norwegian commercial sailing vessel to do so. One reason that this traffic was not found sufficiently profitable was explained in the report in the Montreal *Daily Witness* (7 October 1862), quoted in the Norwegian *Stavanger Amtstidende* (17 November): *Sleipner*'s expenses for tugging and port charges had been close to $1,000, most of them east of Lake Erie, and the Montreal paper observed that it would be necessary to lower costs on the St Lawrence in order to compete with New York. (See Worm-Müller 1935, 574–8).

Bibliography

—— ❖ ——

MANUSCRIPT COLLECTIONS

Collection of immigrant letters. Norsk historisk kjeldeskrift-institutt (NHKI). Oslo.

Jacobson, Abraham. Papers. Norwegian–American Historical Association, St. Olaf College. Northfield, Minn.

Kloster, Asbjørn. Letterbooks 1851–75. Oslo University Library.

GOVERNMENT PUBLICATIONS

Journals of the Legislative Assembly of the Province of Canada.
Sessional Papers of the Parliament of the Province of Canada.

NEWSPAPERS AND JOURNALS

Aftenposten (Oslo)
Almuevennen (Oslo)
Emigranten (Madison, Wisconsin)
Fædrelandet (La Crosse, Wisconsin)
Gazette (Montreal)
Marcus Thrane's Norske Amerikaner (Chicago)
Menneskevennen (Stavanger and Oslo)
Montreal Herald
Morgenbladet (Oslo)
Morning Chronicle and Commercial Shipping Gazette (Quebec)
Quebec Gazette
Sherbrooke Gazette and Eastern Township Advertiser
Skilling–Magazin and its supplement *Ugeskrift for norske Landmænd* (Oslo)
Stavanger Amtstidende og Adresseavis (Stavanger)

Throndhjems–Posten (Trondheim)
Throndhjems Stiftsavis (Trondheim)
Trondhjems Adressecontors–Efterretninger (Trondheim)

BOOKS AND ARTICLES

Bartlett, William Henry. [1842] 1967. *Canadian Scenery Illustrated.* Text by N.P. Willis. London. Facsimile edition. London: Peter Martin Associates Ltd.

Bélanger, Jules, Marc Desjardins, Yves Frenette, and Pierre Dansereau. 1981. *Histoire de la Gaspésie.* Montreal: Boreal Express.

Blegen, Theodore C. 1931. *Norwegian Migration to America 1825–1860.* Northfield, Minn.: The Norwegian–American Historical Association.

– 1940. *Norwegian Migration to America: The American Transition.* Northfield, Minn.: The Norwegian–American Historical Association.

Boyer, George W. 1970. *Early Days in Muskoka: A Story About the Settlement of the Communities in the Free Grant Lands and of Pioneer Life in Muskoka.* Bracebridge, Ont.: Herald–Gazette Press.

Brun, Nils Christian. 1911. "Første aars oplevelser." *Symra* 7: 110–19. Translated by Knute Bergsagel as "My First Years in Canada." In Loken 1980: 273–41.

Caird, James. 1859. *Prairie Farming in America, With Notes by the Way on Canada and the United States.* London. Published in Danish as *Paa Stepperne. Reiseskildringer fra Canada og de Forenede Stater.* 1859. Copenhagen. Edited with an Introduction by Johan Schrøder as "Amerika. Hvor skal Nordboen nu fordelagtigst nedsette sig i denne Verdensdel." 1860. In *Ugeskrift for norske Landmænd* (supplement to *Skilling–Magazin*) 21 (26 May)–29 (21 July).

Canada: A Brief Outline of Her Geographical Position, Productions, Climate, Capabilities, Educational and Municipal Institutions, etc. 1857. Published by Authority. Toronto. Translated into Norwegian by A. Jorgensen as *Canada: En kortfatted skildring af dets geographiske beliggenhed, produkter, klima, beskaffenhed, opdragelses og borgerlige institutioner, etc.* 1857. Toronto. Also in a revised Norwegian edition by Christopher O. Closter. 1861. Stavanger, Norway.

Cowan, Helen I. 1961. *British Emigration to British North America: The First Hundred Years.* Revised and Enlarged Edition. Toronto: University of Toronto Press.

Craig, Gerald M., ed. 1955. *Early Travellers in the Canadas 1791–1867.* Toronto: Macmillan.

Day, C.M. 1869. *History of the Eastern Townships, Province of Quebec, Dominion of Canada, Civil and Descriptive.* Montreal.

Dietrichson, Gustav F. 1861. "Om Udvandringen til Amerika." *Almuevennen* 13, no. 15 (13 April): 115–8 and no. 16 (20 April): 123–5.

Doyle, James, ed. 1980. *Yankees in Canada: A Collection of Nineteenth-Century Travel Narratives.* Downsview, Ont.: ECW Press.

Erickson, Karl E. 1934. Albert O. Barton, ed., "The Emigrant Journey in the Fifties." *Norwegian–American Studies* 8: 65–91.

Fischer, Lewis R., and Helge W. Nordvik. 1985a." A Crucial Six Percent: Norwegian Sailors in the Canadian Merchant Marine, 1863–1913." In *Sjøfartshistorisk Årbok 1984.* Bergen: 139–59.

– 1985b. Peter M. Stuwitz and the Newfoundland Inshore Fishery in 1840. *Newfoundland Studies* 1: 129–40.

Gates, Paul W. 1931. "The Campaign of the Illinois Central Railroad for Norwegian and Swedish Immigrants." *Norwegian–American Studies* 6: 66–88.

– 1934. "Official Encouragement to Immigration by the Province of Canada." *Canadian Historical Review* 15 (March): 24–38.

Gibbs, C.R. Vernon. 1963. *British Passenger Liners of the Five Oceans: A Record of the British Passenger Lines and Their Liners from 1838 to the Present Day.* London: Putnam.

Gilbert, A.G. 1867. *From Montreal to the Maritime Provinces and Back.* Montreal.

Halvorsen, J.B. 1901. *Norsk Forfatter–Lexikon 1814–1880.* Vol. 5. Kristiania.

Harris, R.C., and John Warkentin. 1974. *Canada Before Confederation: A Study in Historical Geography.* London and New York: Oxford University Press.

Hodge, Frederick Webb. [1910] 1969. *Handbook of American Indians North of Mexico* 2 vols. Reprint. New York: Greenwood Press.

Holand, Hjalmar Rued. 1930. "To luftkasteller som blev til pinesteder." In *Den sidste folkevandring: Sagastubber fra nybyggerlivet i Amerika.* Pp. 315–31. Oslo: H. Aschehoug. The chapter on Gaspé was first published as "Gaspe. Et trist blad i vor nybyggersaga." *Symra* 5 (Decorah, Iowa, 1909): 2–8. Translated by Helmer M. Blegen as "Two Air Castles That Turned to Naught." In *Norwegians in America: The Last Migration. Bits of Saga From Pioneer Life.* Pp. 223–33. 1978. Sioux Falls, S. Dak.: Augustana College.

Innis, Mary Quale. 1954. *An Economic History of Canada.* New Ed. Toronto: The Ryerson Press.

Jacobson, Clara. 1929. "Fra svundne Dage." *Reform* (Eau Claire, Wis.) 19 December.

– 1941. "A Journey to America in the Fifties." *Norwegian–American Studies* 12: 60–78.

Jalava, Mauri A. 1983. "The Scandinavians as a Source of Settlers for the Dominion of Canada: The First Generation, 1867–1897." In *Scandinavian–Canadian Studies.* Edited by Edward W. Laine. Ottawa: 5–14.

Johnson, Stanley C. [1913] 1966. *A History of Emigration From the United Kingdom to North America 1763–1912.* London. Reprint. London: Frank Cass.

Jorgensen, A. 1865. *The Emigration from Europe During the Present Century. Its Causes and Effects*. Translated from Norwegian Statistics and Reports and from Extracts of "Histoire de L'Émigration Européenne, Asiatique et Africaine, au XIX Siècle." Quebec.

Knaplund, Paul. 1931. "Norwegians in the Selkirk Settlement 1815–1870." *Norwegian–American Studies* 6: 1–11.

Kohl, Johann Georg. 1861. *Travels in Canada, and Through the States of New York and Pennsylvania*. 2 vols. Translated by Mrs Percy Sinnett from the author's revision of the 1856 German edition. London. An extract in Norwegian translation in *Skilling–Magazin*. Christiania. 1860 (17 Nov.).

Larson, Henrietta. 1928. "An Immigration Journey to America in 1854." *Norwegian–American Studies* 3: 58–64.

Lehmann, Heinz. 1986. *The German Canadians 1750–1957: Immigration, Settlement and Culture*. Translated, edited and introduced by Gerhard P. Bassler. St. John's: Jesperson Press.

Ljungmark, Lars. 1982. "Canada's Campaign for Scandinavian Immigration, 1873–1876." *Swedish–American Historical Quarterly* 33 (January): 21–42.

Loken, Gulbrand. 1980. *From Fjord to Frontier: A History of the Norwegians in Canada*. Toronto: McClelland and Stewart.

Lower, Arthur R.M. 1973. *Great Britain's Woodyard: British America and the Timber Trade, 1763–1867*. Montreal: McGill–Queen's University Press.

Macdonald, Norman. 1966. *Canada: Immigration and Colonization 1841–1903*. Aberdeen: Aberdeen University Press.

Mauralt, J.A. [1866] 1969. *Histoire des Abénakis depuis 1605 jusqu'à nos jours*. Sorel. Reprint. New York: Johnson Reprint Corporation.

Mika, Nick, and Helma Mika. 1981. *Places in Ontario: Their Name Origins and History*. Belleville, Ont.

Morton, W.L. 1964. *The Critical Years: The Union of British North America 1857–1873*. Toronto: McClelland and Stewart.

Murray, Florence B., ed. 1963. *Muskoka and Haliburton 1615–1875: A Collection of Documents*. Toronto: University of Toronto Press.

Nordvik, Helge W. 1988. "Norwegian Emigrants and Canadian Timber: Norwegian Shipping to Quebec 1850–1875." In *Maritime Aspects of Migration*. Edited by Klaus Friedland. Pp. 1–11. Cologne: Böhlau Verlag.

Norlie, Olaf Morgan. 1925. *History of the Norwegian People in America*. Minneapolis: Augsburg Publishing House.

O'Bready, Maurice. 1973. *De Ktiné à Sherbrooke: Esquisse historique de Sherbrooke: des origines à 1954*. Sherbrooke: Université de Sherbrooke.

Øverland, Orm. 1986. "*Skandinaven* and the Beginnings of Professional Publishing." *Norwegian–American Studies* 31: 187–214.

Russell, Loris. 1973. *Everyday Life in Colonial Canada*. London: B.T. Batsford.

Rynning, Ole. 1838. *Sandfærdig Beretning om Amerika, til Oplysning og Nytte for Bonde og Menigmand*. Christiania. Translated and Edited by Theodore C. Blegen as *Ole Rynning's True Account of America*. 1926.

Minneapolis: Norwegian–American Historical Association.

Schrøder, Johan. 1860. *Gaardsregnskab for den norske bonde, et sammen-hengende femaarigt regnskab over navngiven gaard.* Christiania.

– 1863. "En Bog for Nordboerne hjemme og i Amerika." *Emigranten* (Madison, Wis.) 5, 12, 19 October

– 1867. *Skandinaverne i de Forenede Stater og Canada med Indberetninger og Oplysninger fra 200 skandinaviske Settlementer. En Ledetraad for Emigranten fra det gamle Land og for Nybyggeren i Amerika.* La Crosse, Wis.

– 1867. *Skandinaverne i de Forenede Stater og Canada med Indberetninger og Oplysninger fra 200 skandinaviske Settlementer. En Ledetraad for Emigranten fra det gamle Land og for Nybyggeren i Amerika.* Christiania. (In spite of the identical titles, the Christiania edition only includes the chapters on Canada. A projected second volume on the United States was never published.)

– 1868. *Vägvisare för Emigranter till Förenta Staterna och Canada. Anvisningar beträffande resan dit, de olika staternas klimat, jordmån och öfriga förhållanden, meddelanden från talrika skandinaviska nybyggare, m.m.* Stockholm.

– 1893. *Costa Rica. Immigration Pamphlet with Two Maps: A Guide for the Agricultural Class Coming from Other Countries to Make Costa Rica its Home.* Published by Order of the Supreme Government of Costa Rica. San José, Costa Rica.

Semmingsen, Ingrid. 1941. *Veien mot vest: Utvandringen fra Norge til Amerika 1825–1865.* Oslo: H. Aschehoug.

– 1950. *Veien mot vest: Utvandringen fra Norge 1865–1915.* Oslo: H. Aschehoug.

Skilling, H. Gordon. 1945. *Canadian Representation Abroad: From Agency to Embassy.* Toronto: The Ryerson Press.

Sollid, A. 1896. *En Amerikatur. Reiseerindringer.* Skien, Norway.

Stafford, Kate, and Harald Naess, eds. 1984. *On Both Sides of the Ocean: A Part of Per Hagen's Journey.* Northfield, Minn.: The Norwegian–American Historical Association.

Stangeland, Elias. 1853. *Nogle veiledende Vink for norske Udvandrere til Amerika.* Christiania.

Sturz, Johann Jakob. 1860. *Plan for Securing to British North–America a Larger Share than Heretofore it has Received, of the Emigration from the United Kingdom as well as from Germany and also from other Countries of Europe …* Berlin.

Trigger, Bruce G., ed. 1978. *Northeast.* Vol. 15 of *Handbook of North American Indians.* Washington, D.C.: Smithsonian Institution.

Wick. B.L. 1914. "Den første koloni i Gaspé, Quebec." *Samband* (Minneapolis) 5, no. 80 (December): 103–6.

Wicklund, A. 1967. Ætta Tambs. Fana, Norway. Typescript.

Worm-Müller, Jacob S. 1935. "Emigrant-og Kanadafarten." In vol. 2, part 1, of *Den norske sjøfarts historie fra de ældste tider til vore dager.* Pp. 547–635. Oslo: Steenske forlag.

Index

—— ·:· ——